Indian Knowledge System (IKS) Series

OCCAM

The Ramayana School

Knowledge Partner

# Ramayana for Every Child

## Taking Rama to Every Home

Shantanu Gupta

Typsetting: Syed Dilshad Ali



ISBN: 978-93-65474-80-0

First published in India 2025
This edition published 2025

Published by
BluOne Ink Pvt. Ltd
A-76, 2nd Floor, Sector 136, Noida
Uttar Pradesh 201305

Website: www.bluone.ink
Email: publisher@bluone.ink

Printed and bound in India at Nutech Print Services - India

Kali and Occam are imprints of BluOne Ink

# Ramayana for Every Child

## Taking Rama to Every Home

Shantanu Gupta

We believe that this book is blessed by Sri Rama and protected by Hanuman ji.

This book belongs to ______________________________.

# CONTENT

# From the Author's Desk

Namastey parents and children!

While our education system continues to prioritize utilitarian learning, with a strong emphasis on EdTech apps for teaching Mathematics, Science, Coding, and similar subjects, I felt a pressing need for value-based education. This approach would throw light on concepts like resilience, honesty, kindness, compassion, truthfulness, conflict resolution, and stress management—skills that are crucial in navigating the relentless challenges of today's world.

Rarely do we encounter a framework that fosters the art of robust decision making. The life-long pursuit of a high intelligence quotient (IQ) often leaves us and our children deficient in emotional quotient (EQ). While high IQ may propel us to excel in our careers, low EQ can undermine our ability to cope with the multifaceted demands of modern life, leading to struggles far beyond professional success.

Even as a super smart coder, a brilliant scientist, a top-notch business brain, or a world-renowned doctor, life will continue to present us with complicated emotional conflicts. Are we preparing our children to deal with such situations adequately? This book is an endeavour to make learning the story of Ramayana fun for children and families. It attempts to enable families to explore the Ramayana together through puzzles, quizzes, games, and other activities.

Rama spent 14 years in exile, demonstrating unparalleled grit and determination. These years tested him with some of the harshest challenges imaginable. Once destined to become the king of the mighty Kosala empire, he was instead banished to the forest. After enduring nearly 13 years of hardships, his wife, Sita, was kidnapped, pushing him into a life-threatening war against the mighty army of Ravana. Rama lost his kingdom, his wife, and almost his life during the war. Yet, despite these trials, he did not take any shortcuts. He did not return to his brother Bharata for assistance, nor did he compromise his honesty, goodness, or righteousness. After the initial agony of Sita's abduction, he calmed himself, relying on the skills he learnt from his teachers.

Rama strategized with the resources available to him and forged local alliances. Hanuman helped him search for Sita, Angad helped him in a diplomatic peace mission, Jambavan helped him keep the team motivated, engineers Nala and Neel helped him build the Rama Bridge across the sea to Lanka, and Vibhishana helped him penetrate the secrets of the opposition army. In the end, Rama and his Vanara army won against the mighty Ravana and his resourceful, well-equipped army.

*Ramayana for Every Child* is a one-of-a-kind book that explains "Bala Kanda" to "Yudh Kanda" through puzzles, games, art exercises, quizzes, and reflective exercises. The story of each *kanda*—Bala Kanda, Ayodhya Kanda, Aranya Kanda, Kishkinda Kanda, Sunder Kanda, and Yudh Kanda—is presented in brief paragraphs in a fill in the keywords format. This is followed by 40 multiple choice questions to help children remember the key characters, places, and incidents of that *kanda*.

Every *kanda* also has an original, coloured artwork to enable children visualize the story while reading it. After understanding the story of Ramayana through the fill in the blanks and quiz challenges, children can engage with sequencing puzzles, maze puzzles, crosswords, word search puzzles, Madhubani art colouring activities, and emoji puzzles. An answer key is provided at the end of the book.

This book has come to life with the help of many friends and colleagues.

Priyanka Sharma helped me with content research.

Pallavi Saxena and Anand Upadhaya helped design the book.

Deepti Agarwal Mittal helped with the Madhubani artwork and Krunal Gohel and his team helped with the other artwork for the book.

My family pitched in too: My wife Swetha Rao Duggu helped edit the book, and my children Abhiram and Tara helped me review the book from a children's perspective.

Throughout the book, you will find multiple spellings for the same character, such as Lakshmana and Laxmana, and Bali and Vali. This has been done intentionally; all versions are correct and have been purposely used to familiarize the reader with the different acceptable spellings for each of the names.

This unique book on Indian *itihasa* is designed for children, teaching the Ramayana in a scholastic yet engaging way. It incorporates critical thinking, visual thinking, art-based learning, vocabulary building, and reflective exercises through puzzles and activities. Aligned with the National Education Policy (NEP) of the Government of India, which emphasizes the Indian knowledge system (IKS), this book serves as a valuable contribution to fostering cultural and educational enrichment.

This is Ramayana for every child and every family.

Jai Sri Ram!

# A Learn Ramayana

Explore the Story of

# Bal Kanda

# 1

# Fill in the blanks to complete the tale from Rama's birth to his marriage to Mata Sita.

King Dasharatha was the king of the Kosala Empire, and Ayodhya was the capital of the empire. The king had three queens: (a) __________, (b) ______________, and (c) __________. Since he did not have any children who could succeed him on the throne, he performed a special fire sacrifice called the (d) _____________ Yagna. From this fire, a deity named Yagna Purush appeared and gave King Dasharatha a vessel of milk pudding called payasam, instructing him to share it among his three wives.

After some time, Kausalya gave birth to (e) ___________, Sumitra to the twins (f) __________ and (g) __________ , and Kaikeyi to (h) __________. All four brothers began their training under the wise Rishi Vashishtha.

One day, Rishi (i) __________ came to visit King Dasharatha. He needed Rama and Laxmana's help to protect his Yagnas from two troublesome demons, (j) ___________ and (k) __________. Dasharatha was a little reluctant as Rama and Laxmana were still young. But with a heavy heart, King Dasharatha agreed and sent his two sons with the rishi.

On their journey, they encountered a demoness named (l) __________, whom Rama bravely defeated. On the final day of the six-day Yagna, the two demons attacked the Yagna with their group of mischief-makers. With one arrow, Rama sent (m) __________ far into the sea. With another arrow, he killed (n) __________.

After the demons were vanquished, Rishi Vishwamitra, along with the two princes, travelled to Mithila, the capital city of Videha. (o) __________ was the king of Mithila and the father of Sita. The king decided to hold a swayamvara (a ceremony where the girl chooses her spouse), where the challenge was to lift the mighty bow of (p) ________. No one could even budge it. Following Rishi Vishwamitra's advice, (q) _________ easily lifted the bow. As he began to string it, the bow broke with a loud crash, and he won the challenge.

In the end, the young couple were married happily.

# 2

# Bal Kanda Quiz

1. **Who wrote the original Ramayana?**
   a) Rishi Vashisht
   b) Rishi Valmiki
   c) Rishi Ved Vyas
   d) Rishi Vishwa Mitra
2. **How many sargas (chapters) are there in Valmiki Ramayana?**
   a) 108
   b) 1,008
   c) 645
   d) 202
3. **How many shlokas are there in Valmiki Ramayana?**
   a) 24,000
   b) 1,00,000
   c) 1,008
   d) 645
4. **Whose avatar was Lord Rama?**
   a) Bhagwan Bhrama
   b) Bhagwan Vishnu
   c) Bhagwan Shiva
   d) Bhagwan Krishna
5. **In the chronological order of Lord Vishnu's avataras (incarnations), which number is Rama?**
   a) 5
   b) 7
   c) 6
   d) 8
6. **In which language is Valmiki Ramayana written?**
   a) Awadhi
   b) Prakrat
   c) Sanskrit
   d) Pali

**7. Ayodhya was built on the banks of which river?**

a) Yamuna
b) Ganga
c) Sarayu
d) Sarasvati

**8. The Kingdom of Kosala belonged to which dynasty?**

a) Gupta Dynasty
b) Chola Dynasty
c) Maurya Dynasty
d) Surya Dynasty

**9. Who established the city of Ayodhya?**

a) King Manu
b) King Ishvaku
c) King Bhaghirath
d) King Raghu

**10. Who was the kul guru of Ayodhya during King Dashratha's reign?**

a) Sage Vasishtha
b) Sage Valmiki
c) Sage Ved-Vyas
d) Sage Braghu

**11. Valmiki Ramayana is part of which text in the Indian Knowledge System?**

a) Vedas
b) Upanishadas
c) Puranas
d) Itihasa

**12. King Dashratha had three wives: Kaushalya, Kaikeyi, and ________________.**

a) Kalyani
b) Sumitra
c) Kalpita
d) Sumana

**13. In which nakshatra was Rama was born?**

a) Magha
b) Mool
c) Punarvasu
d) Ashwani

14. **Who was Bhagwan Rama's mother?**
    a) Sumitra
    b) Kaushalya
    c) Kaikeyi
    d) Anasuya

15. **Which yagna did King Dashratha perform to be blessed with a child?**
    a) Maha Ganapathy Homam
    b) Sudarsana Homam
    c) Ayush Homam
    d) Putra Kameshti Yagna

16. **Which rishi did King Dashrath invite to perform the yagna?**
    a) Rishi Valmiki
    b) Rishi Rishyasringa
    c) Rishi Bharadwaj
    d) Rishi Atri

17. **Who came to Ayodhya to request Rama and Laxmana to accompany him in defeating the *rakshasas*?**
    a) Rishi Vasishtha
    b) Rishi Valmiki
    c) Rishi Ved-Vyas
    d) Rishi Vishwamitra

18. **Which Kosala King brought the revered River Ganga to earth?**
    a) Sagar
    b) Bhageeratha
    c) Dilipa
    d) Dashrath

19. **What gift did Yagna Purush give to King Dasharatha during the Putra Kameshti yagna?**
    a) A magical bow
    b) A vessel of *payasam* (milk pudding)
    c) A golden chariot
    d) A jewel-encrusted crown

20. **What is the name of the Kingdom of Bhagwan Rama?**
    a) Kingdom of Ayodhya
    b) Kingdom of Kosala

c) Kingdom of Surya
d) Kingdom of Manu

**21. What was the capital of the Kingdom of Kosala?**
a) Ayodhya
b) Kosala
c) Patliputra
d) Delhi

**22. In which Indian state is the city of Ayodhya located today?**
a) Madhya Pradesh
b) Kosala
c) Uttarakhand
d) Uttar Pradesh

**23. Who was the first demon or demoness killed by Lord Rama?**
a) Mareech
b) Subaho
c) Tadaka
d) Khar

**24. Who cursed Devi Ahalya to turn into a rock?**
a) Rishi Gautam
b) Rishi Vashishtha
c) Rishi Bhardwaj
d) Rishi Vishwamitra

**25. Who ruled Mithila during the time of King Dashrath?**
a) King Ishvaku
b) King Raghu
c) King Janaka
d) King Bhagirath

**26. Which Hindu festival is celebrated on the occasion of the birth of Sri Rama?**
a) Deepawali
b) Dussehra
c) Rama Navami
d) Holi

**27. Janka was the king of which kingdom?**
a) Ayodhya
b) Mithila
c) Indraprastha
d) Vijyanagar

**28. Bhagwan Parashurama is the incarnation of____________________?**

a) Bhagwan Krishna
b) Bhagwan Vishnu
c) Bhagwan Shiva
d) Bhagwan Indra

**29. What was the name of Laxamana's wife?**

a) Urvashi
b) Urmila
c) Menala
d) Meenakshi

**30. Which demon, after being cast away by Rama's arrows, later returned to create trouble for him?**

a) Khar
b) Vatapi
c) Mareech
d) Indrajeet

**31. Who became very angry when Rama broke Shiva's *dhanush* (bow)?**

a) King Ravana
b) King Dashrath
c) Bhagwan Parashuram
d) Bhagwan Indra

**32. Which of the following vows did Rama take for life?**

a) To be the king of the universe
b) To establish his power in Ayodhya
c) Eka Patni Vrata (One Life, One Wife)
d) To kill Ravana and destroy Lanka

**33. Who was Shatrughan's wife?**

a) Suhasa
b) Suveni
c) Sruthakeerthi
d) Suhasini

**34. Who was Bharat's wife?**

a) Mandavi
b) Mandodari
c) Menaka
d) Meenakshi

**35. Who gifted Kanak Bhawan to Rama and Sita after their marriage?**

a) Sunaina
b) Kaikeyi
c) Sumitra
d) Kausalya

**36. During his exile, Guha helped Rama cross which river?**

a) Sarayu
b) Ganga
c) Yamuna
d) Kaveri

**37. Who was Mareech's mother?**

a) Surpanakha
b) Tadaka
c) Mandodari
d) Ruma

**38. In which *kanda* of Valmiki Ramayana was Mata Sita kidnapped?**

a) Ayodhya Kand
b) Sundar Kand
c) Aranya Kand
d) Kishkindha Kand

**39. Who was King Dasharatha's eldest son?**

a) Bharata
b) Laxmana
c) Rama
d) Shatrughna

**40. In which *kanda* of Valmiki Ramayana was Lord Rama sent to exile—*vanvasa*?**

a) Ayodhya Kand
b) Bal Kand
c) Aranya Kand
d) Khishkinda Kand

# NAME ALL THE THE AVTARS OF BHAGWAN VISHNU

1.

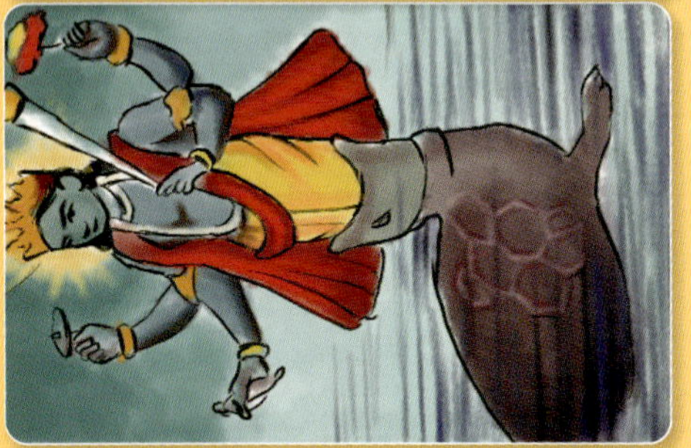

2.

3.

4.

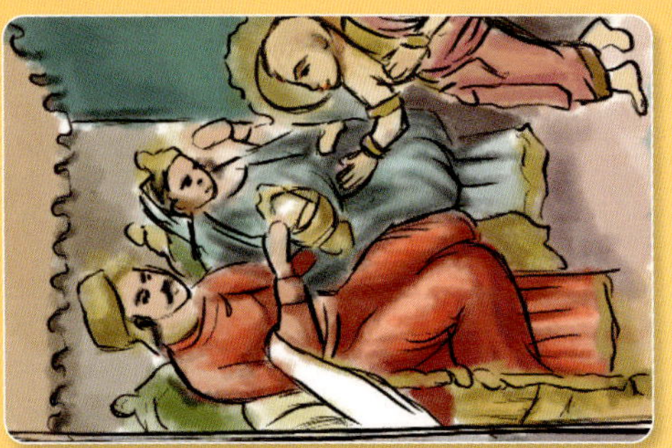

5.

6.

7.

8.

9.

10.

Check answers on page 148

Explore the Story of

# Ayodhya Kanda

# 3

# Fill in the blanks to complete the tale of Rama's exile.

By now, Rama, Laxamana, Bharata, and Shatrughna were married and trained in various aspects of statecraft. King Dasharatha was growing old and keen to choose his successor. After consultations with his court men, kings of neighbouring kingdoms, his people's representatives, and (a) __________, one name emerged unanimously as best suited to take over the kingdom.

(b) ______________, feeling glad after hearing the words of the assembled people, requested sage Vasishtha to begin arrangements for the (c) ______________ ceremony of the new king. After informing the young prince of the people's desire for him to be king, Dasharatha advised him on how to govern the kingdom for the well-being of the people.

Everyone was thrilled about the upcoming ceremony, except (d) ___________ who was upset at and jealous of the king-to-be. This person told (e) __________ about the prince's upcoming ascension to the throne. On hearing about the new king, the latter was delighted and handed over one of her jewels as well. But her mind was poisoned by this wicked and jealous person who left no stone unturned in talking about the misfortunes that would befall her family if this prince became the new king of the empire.

Convinced with the brainwashing, she then asked King Dasharatha to fulfil two of her (f) _________: first was to crown (g) ______________ as the new king of Ayodhya and second was to send (h) __________ to (i) __________ years of exile. Dasharatha, in deep pain, asked the chosen one to leave, who obediently accepted his father's orders and left Ayodhya along with (j) ________ and (k) _________.

(l) ___________, a Nishad chieftain, met the three on their way to exile, paid his respect to them, and helped them cross the river (m) ___________. A few months after Rama left, Dasharatha died out of grief and sorrow. Bharata then reached the city of Ayodhya and confronted his mother (n) ___________. When he returned to Ayodhya, he found the kingdom in utmost pain and sorrow. Bharata promised that he would bring his brother (o) _______ back to Ayodhya.

(p) _________ informed Bharata about his brother's initial route during the exile. Bharata then approached Rishi (q) ____________ and requested him to share the exact location of the exiled prince's new abode in the forest. Bharata reached (r) _________ and requested his brother to return to Ayodhya and accept the (s) __________.

The noble prince, however, refused to return with Bharata. He asked Bharata to take care of the kingdom of Ayodhya in his absence. Bharata returned, carrying his brother's *kadhau* (sandals), which he placed on the throne. He ruled Ayodhya as his brother's representative from (t) _____________, a small village away from the city.

# 4 Ayodhya Kanda Quiz

1. **Why did Dashratha choose Rama to be the king of Ayodhya?**
   a) Rama was the eldest son.
   b) Rama's qualities of leadership and care were appreciated by everyone.
   c) Rama was the only trained warrior.
   d) Rama was the favourite of Dashratha.

2. **What is the origin of Queen Kaikeyi's name?**
   a) Her father's name was Kekaya.
   b) Her father was the king of the Kekeya kingdom.
   c) She came from a crab (*kekada*).
   d) She was cursed by a crow (*kak*).

3. **Who was the king of Kekeya kingdom and the father of Kaikeyi?**
   a) Janak
   b) Ashwathama
   c) Ashwapati
   d) Bhagirath

4. **Who poisoned Rani Kaikeyi's mind, prompting her to ask King Dasharatha to send Lord Rama to exile?**
   a) Menaka
   b) Bharat
   c) Tadaka
   d) Manthara

5. **What were the two boons that Rani Kaikeyi asked King Dashratha for?**
   a) *Vanvasa* for Rama and *vanvasa* for Laxman
   b) *Vanvasa* for Rama and kingship for Bharata
   c) *Vanvasa* for Sita and *vanvasa* for Laxman
   d) *Vanvasa* for Rama and kingship for Laxman

6. **Who was enraged on hearing about Rama's exile?**
   a) Sumantra
   b) Dasaratha
   c) Laxaman
   d) Sita

7. **Who accompanied Rama on his exile?**
   a) Bharat and Sita
   b) Laxman and Sita
   c) Laxman and Bharat
   d) Bharat and Shatrughan

8. **Who from King Dashratha's court accompanied Rama, Sita, and Laxaman to the outskirts of Ayodhya?**
   a) Sumantra
   b) Rishi Vashisht
   c) Guha
   d) Shatrughan

9. **Who helped Rama, Sita, and Laxaman cross River Sarayu?**
   a) Sumantra
   b) Guha
   c) Bharat
   d) Rishi Bhardawaj

10. **Which rishi's ashram did Rama, Sita, and Laxaman first reach during their exile (vanvas)?**
   a) Rishi Valmiki
   b) Rishi Bhardawaj
   c) Rishi Atri
   d) Rishi Vishwa Mitra

11. **By which river did Rama spend his first night after leaving Ayodhya for the vanvas?**
   a) Ganga
   b) Tamasa
   c) Yamuna
   d) Godavari

12. **Where did Ram and Bharat meet during Rama's exile?**
   a) Panchvati
   b) Kishkinda
   c) Chitrakoot
   d) Lanka

13. **Whom did King Dashratha mistakenly kill while hunting in the forest?**
   a) Sumantra
   b) Subahu
   c) Mareech
   d) Shravana Kumar

**14. When Bharat was going to meet his elder brother Rama in the jungle, what did Guha, Rishi Bharadwaj, and Laxmana think about Bharat's intentions?**

a) ... that Bharat was going to convince Rama to return to Ayodhya.
b) ... that Bharat was going to kill Rama so he could never return.
c) ... that Bharat was going to discuss how to rule Ayodhya in Rama's absence.
d) ... that Bharat was going to discuss King Dhashratha's demise.

**15. On Rama's refusal to return to Ayodhya, Bharata said, "I shall sit and fast here till Rama agrees to come back to Ayodhya." Who gave the suggestion to break this deadlock?**

a) Kaushalya
b) Kaikeyi
c) Rishi Vasishtha
d) Bharat himself

**16. How did Bharata rule Ayodhya, after meeting Rama at Chitrakoot?**

a) With Rama's *padukas* (sandals) on the throne, Bharata lived in a hut in a village.
b) With Rama's *padukas* (sandals) on the throne, Bharata lived inside the palace.
c) As Rama's representative sitting on the throne, but he lived in a hut in a village.
d) As Rama's representative sitting on the throne, but he lived inside the palace.

**17. What did Rama do to prevent the people of Ayodhya from following him into the forest?**

a) Asked his charioteer to break the chariot
b) Asked his charioteer to fly the chariot
c) Asked his charioteer to burn the chariot
d) Asked his charioteer to create multiple misleading tyre marks of the chariot

**18. Who guided Rama, Sita, and Laxamana to settle in Chitrakoot?**

a) Rishi Valmiki
b) Sumantra
c) Rishi Bhardawaj
d) Guha

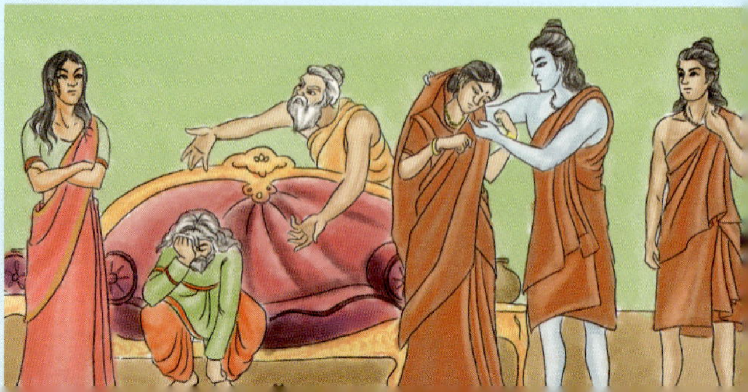

**19. What was the reaction of the people of Ayodhya upon hearing about Rama's exile?**

a) They celebrated the decision.
b) They remained indifferent.
c) They expressed sorrow and tried to follow him.
d) They sided with Kaikeyi.

**20. After Rama, Sita, and Laxmana went into exile, which past mistake did Dasharatha share with Queen Kaushalya?**

a) When Dashratha killed a deer
b) When Dashratha killed Shravana Kumar
c) When Dashratha did injustice in his court
d) When Dashratha gave two boons to Kaikeyi

**21. After Dashrath's death, what did Rishi Vasishtha do?**

a) Install himself as the king of Ayodhya
b) Install Sumantra as the king of Ayodhya
c) Sent messengers to call for Bharat and Shatrughan
d) Sent messengers to call for Rama and Laxmana

**22. Where were Bharat and Shatrughan at the time of Rama's exile?**

a) Away at their maternal grandfather's home at Kekeya
b) Away for some administrative work in Mithila
c) At the palace in Ayodhya
d) In the forest with Rishi Vishwamitra

**23. Who accompanied Bharata to the forest when he went to meet Rama?**

a) No one
b) A few army men
c) A large number of citizens, army, gurus, ministers, and all the family members
d) Only Shatrughna

**24. How did Rama react to the news of King Dashratha's death?**

a) He fainted in sorrow and grief.
b) He stopped talking.
c) He did not react at all.
d) He got angry.

**25. Along with Bharata, which rishi tried to persuade Rama to give up his vow of exile and accept the crown of Ayodhya?**

a) Rishi Vashisht
b) Rishi Vishwamitra
c) Rishi Valmiki
d) Rishi Jabali

**26. After returning from Chitrakoot, where did Bharata live in Ayodhya?**
- a) In the palace in Ayodhya
- b) In a village named Nandigrama near Ayodhya
- c) In a village named Patliputra
- d) In a village named Ayodhyapuram

**27. After leaving Chitrakoot, whose ashram did Rama, Sita, and Laxmana visit first?**
- a) Rishi Atri
- b) Rishi Bharadwaj
- c) Rishi Vashishtha
- d) Rishi Valmiki

**28. Name Rishi Atri's wife, who blessed Mata Sita with divine ornaments?**
- a) Anasuya
- b) Ahalya
- c) Maneka
- d) Mandodari

**29. What did Mata Anasuya teach Mata Sita?**
- a) To use weapons
- b) To play the role of a devoted wife
- c) To find food in a jungle
- d) To make a house in a jungle

**30. Which *kanda* follows Ayodhya Kanda?**
- a) Sundar Kanda
- b) Kishkindha Kanda
- c) Aranya Kanda
- d) Yudh Kanda

**31. What did Rama do to reassure the people of Ayodhya before his departure?**
- a) He held a grand assembly to address them.
- b) He promised to return within a year.
- c) He gave them a speech about his duty and honour.
- d) He escaped without talking to the people of Ayodhya.

**32. Today, there is a temple in Chitrakoot exactly at the same place where Bharata met Rama during the exile. What is the temple called?**
- a) Bharat Milap Temple
- b) Bharat Khoj Temple
- c) Raja Bharat Temple
- d) Mel-Jol Temple

**33. Who rescued King Dasharatha in the battle against Asura Shambara?**
  a) Sumantra
  b) Indra
  c) Kaikeyi
  d) Rama

**34. Who/what adorned the throne of Ayodhya for 14 long years in Rama's absence?**
  a) Bharat
  b) Rama's bow and arrow
  c) Rama's ring
  d) Rama's *charan paduka* (sandals)

**35. What did Kaikeyi's maid Manthara say to manipulate her into demanding Rama's exile?**
  a) Flattery about her beauty
  b) Stories of past kings
  c) Fear of losing power and status
  d) Promises of riches and wealth

**36. Sri Rama is the incarnation of Bhagwan Vishnu. Whose incarnation is Laxmana?**
  a) Shesha Naga, the snake that sheltered Bhagwan Vishnu
  b) Vishnu's conch shell
  c) Vishnu's mace
  d) Sudarshana Chakra, Vishnu's weapon

**37. Who was Laxmana's twin brother?**
  a) Sri Rama
  b) Shatrughna
  c) Bharata
  d) Guha

**38. In which Indian state is Chitrakoot located today, where Rama and Bharata met during Rama's exile?**
  a) Karnataka
  b) Uttar Pradesh
  c) Maharashtra
  d) Uttarakhand

**39. How did Rama react when he was asked to go into exile?**
  a) He screamed at Kaikeyi.
  b) He argued with Dashratha.
  c) He respectfully accepted his father's order.
  d) He denied to go into exile.

**40. In which *kanda* of Valmiki Ramayana was Mata Sita was kidnapped by Ravana?**

a) Ayodhya Kanda
b) Yudha Kanda
c) Aranya Kanda
d) Sundar Kanda

# NAME THESE 3 RAMAYANA CHARACTERS

1.

2.

3.

Check answers on page 148

Explore the Story of

# Aranya Kanda

# 5 Fill in the blanks to complete the tale of Rama's exile.

After Bharat left Chitrakoot, Rama also decided to move on from there. After moving from one guru's ashram to another in search of knowledge and wisdom in the formidable jungle of Dandakaranya for almost 12 years, Rama was advised by Rishi (a) ____________ to spend the remaining time of his exile in (b) ____________. Rama moved to Panchavati after a long journey through Dandaka forest and gradually settled there with Sita and Laxmana.

One day, a demoness named (c) ____________ was passing through and noticed Rama and Laxmana. She was charmed by Rama's personality and approached him in the disguise of a beautiful lady, asking him to (d) ____________ her. Rama outrightly refused her offer, stating that he was already married and had taken *eka patni vrata*, meaning the one-life, one-wife vow. After Rama's refusal, she approached Laxmana with the same proposal, but he too rejected her.

Disappointed and humiliated, Surpanakha noticed Sita and presumed her to be the reason for Rama's refusal. In her outrage, she ferociously attempted to attack Sita. Laxmana treated Mata Sita as his mother, and ensuring Rama and Sita's safety was his primary goal. Laxmana was unable to tolerate the sight of Sita being attacked. In a sudden rage, Laxmana cut off Surpanakha's (e) ____________.

The bleeding Surpanakha ran to her brothers, (f) ____________ and ____________ and narrated the whole incident. The brothers then marched towards Panchavati and attacked Rama and Laxamana.

The result was no surprise; the two attackers were killed in battle. Then Shurpanakha fled to (g) __________ and demanded revenge for the insults she had faced.

Surpanakha's benefactor agreed to teach Ram a lesson by kidnapping his wife Sita. He asked (h) __________ to become a golden deer and attract Sita with its beauty. Expectedly, Sita was lured by the deer and requested Ram to catch it for her immediately.

During the chase, the deer took Rama far into the jungle. Ultimately Rama killed the deer but before dying it cried for help in Rama's voice, prompting Sita to request Laxmana to go help Rama. Laxmana secured Sita by encircling her with a line, famously known as Laxmana (i) __________ that no one could cross. He instructed her not to cross that line at any cost.

When Surpanakha's evil benefactor found Sita alone, he approached her in the disguise of a hermit. He earnestly asked for food and made Sita cross the line and kidnapped her. Meanwhile, (j) __________ heard Sita's screams and immediately followed Ravana. Though the demigod tried to challenge the demon bravely, he succumbed. When his wings were severed, he fell back on earth. Despite his pain and agony, he held onto life until he was able to give Rama and Laxmana two crucial clues and tell them who had kidnapped Sita. He also informed them that Sita was taken towards the (k) __________.

# 6 Aranya Kanda Quiz

1. **After how many years of stay in the Dandaka forest did Lord Rama reach the hermitage of the saint Agastya?**
   a) 12
   b) 18
   c) 10
   d) 8
2. **In which forest did Rama, Sita, and Laxaman spend most of their time during the exile?**
   a) Chambal forest
   b) Kishkinda
   c) Dandaka forest
   c) Jim Corbett
3. **Who advised Rama, Sita, and Laxaman to settle in Panchavati for the rest of their exile?**
   a) Rishi Valmiki
   b) Rishi Agastya
   c) Rishi Vashishth
   d) Rishi Durvasa
4. **Panchvati is called Panchvati, because _________**
   a) it has 5 banyan trees.
   b) it has 5 rudraksha trees.
   c) it has 5 cave houses.
   d) it has 5 tree houses.
5. **While living in Panchavati, which river's water did Rama, Sita, and Laxmana use?**
   a) Ganga
   b) Yamuna
   c) Godavari
   d) Sarayu

6. **In which state of India is Panchavati located?**
   a) Maharashtra
   b) Madhya Pradesh
   c) Andhra Pradesh
   d) Uttar Pradesh

7. **Which demoness attacked Mata Sita, prompting Laxmana to cut off her nose and ears in response?**
   a) Tadaka
   b) Mareech
   c) Surpanakha
   d) Khar

8. **Which rakshasa duo and their massive army first came to fight with Rama and Laxmana after the Surpanakha incident?**
   a) Indrajeet-Kumbhkaran
   b) Khara-Dushan
   c) Mareech-Subaho
   d) Tadaka-Surpanakha

9. **Who came in the disguise of a golden deer to attract Mata Sita?**
   a) Ravana
   b) Subaho
   c) Mareech
   d) Khar

10. **From which place did Ravan kidnap Mata Sita?**
   a) Panchavati
   b) Chitrakoot
   c) Kishkinda
   d) Lanka

11. **What disguise did Ravana use to kidnap Mata Sita?**
   a) Black deer
   b) Begging hermit
   c) Eagle
   d) Golden deer

12. **Who tried to save Mata Sita when Ravana was taking her away to Lanka?**
   a) Garuda
   b) Sampati
   c) Jatayu
   d) Hanuman

13. **What were the two important clues about Mata Sita's abduction that Jatayu shared with Rama and Laxmana before he died?**
    a) Ravana abducted her and took her to Lanka.
    b) Ravana abducted her and took her towards the north.
    c) Ravana abducted her and took her towards the south.
    d) Mareech abducted her and took her to Lanka.

14. **While departing, what did Rishi Agastya gift Rama?**
    a) A sword
    b) A mantra
    c) Arrows
    d) Divine herbs

15. **Who was Surpanakha's father?**
    a) Ghatotkach
    b) Vishrava Muni
    c) Mareech
    d) Vatapi

16. **By refusing Surpanakha's marriage proposal, what larger message did Rama convey?**
    a) Message of bravery
    b) Message in favour of monogamy
    c) Message of smartly insulting others
    d) Message of how to live in a jungle

17. **How large was Khara and Dooshan's army?**
    a) 14 demons
    b) 140 demons
    c) 1,400 demons
    d) 14,000 demons

18. **What was Mareech's reaction on listening to Ravana's plan of kidnapping Mata Sita?**
    a) Mareech loved the idea.
    b) Mareech warned Ravana against adducting Sita.
    c) Mareech ran away.
    d) Mareech fainted.

19. **Which bird fought ferociously with Ravana to resist Sita's abduction?**
    a) Sampati
    b) Aruna
    c) Garuda
    d) Jatayu

**20. Ravana sought whose help to abduct Sita?**
a) Khara and Dooshan
b) Bali
c) Surpanakha
d) Mareech

**21. Who was the first to warn Ravana against meddling with Rama?**
a) Khara
b) Tadaka
c) Mareech
d) Surpanakha

**22. Name the demon who captured Rama and Laxmana while they were searching for Mata Sita in the forest?**
a) Khara
b) Dooshan
c) Mareech
d) Kabandha

**23. After the abduction of Mata Sita, who pacified the angry Rama to not destroy the whole world because of the bad deed of one person?**
a) Rishi Agastya
b) Laxmana
c) Rishi Suteekeshna
d) Jatayu

**24. Kabandha advised Rama to go towards Rishimukha hills to meet __________.**
a) Hanumana
b) Sugreeva
c) Bali
d) Ravana

**25. Panchavati is located by which river?**
a) Ganga
b) Krishna
c) Godavari
d) Narmada

**26. Who was Jatayu's father?**

a) Aruna
b) Sun
c) Indra
d) Sampati

**27. Who became suspicious when Mata Sita was fascinated by the golden deer and asked Rama to fetch it for her?**

a) Laxmana
b) Rama
c) Mareech
d) Jatayu

**28. Ravana asked ____________ to take the form of a beautiful ___________ with silver spots and jewelled horns and roam in the vicinity of ______________ to attract Mata Sita. Fill in the blanks.**

a) Mareech, golden deer, Panchvati
b) Jatayu, golden swan, Dandaka
c) Khar, golden swan, Dandaka
d) Jatayu, golden swan, Kishkinda

**29. What did Ravana decide when Surpanakha told him that Sita was the most beautiful woman in the world?**

a) Ravana decided to kill Rama and Laxmana.
b) Ravana decided to ignore this fact.
c) Ravana decided to abduct Sita.
d) Ravana decided to punish Surpanakha.

**30. Which old *tapaswini* offered half-eaten fruits to Lord Rama?**

a) Guha's wife
b) Shabari
c) Devi Ahilya
d) Mandodari

**31. Why did the old *tapaswini* offer half-eaten fruits to Lord Rama?**

a) She was very hungry.
b) She wanted to check the sweetness of the fruits before offering them.

c) She got lost in Rama's presence.
d) She was very old.

**32. Who killed Jatayu?**
a) Ravana
b) Rama
c) Mareech
d) Subhau

**33. Walking towards which lake did Rama and Laxmana meet Mata Shabari?**
a) Chilika Lake
b) Pangong Lake
c) Pampa Lake
d) Sardar Sarovar Lake

**34. How many eyes did the demon Kabandha have?**
a) 3 eyes
b) 4 eyes
c) 1 eye
d) 2 eyes

**35. Who relieved Kabandha from his curse?**
a) Sugreev
b) Hanuman
c) Rama
d) Bali

**36. What does Rama do when he first encounters Shabari?**
a) He ignores her.
b) He accepts her hospitality.
c) He criticizes her food.
d) He asks for guidance.

**37. Who performed the funeral rites of Jatayu?**
a) Hanuman
b) Kabandha
c) Sampati
d) Rama

**38. Where was the head of the demon Kabandha located on his body?**
a) Stomach
b) Throat
c) Chest
d) None of the above

**39. What did Shabri do after seeing Rama and offering him half-eaten fruits?**

a) She went deep inside the jungle.
b) She went into deep meditation.
c) She sat on the funeral pyre.
d) She went along with Rama and Laxmana.

**40. In which *kanda* do Rama and Laxmana meet Hanuman and Sugriva?**

a) Bala Kanda
b) Kishkinda Kanda
c) Ayodhya Kanda
d) Yudha Kanda

## NAME THESE 4 RAMAYANA CHARACTERS

1.

2.

3.

4.

Check answers on page 148

Explore the Story of

# Kishkinda Kanda

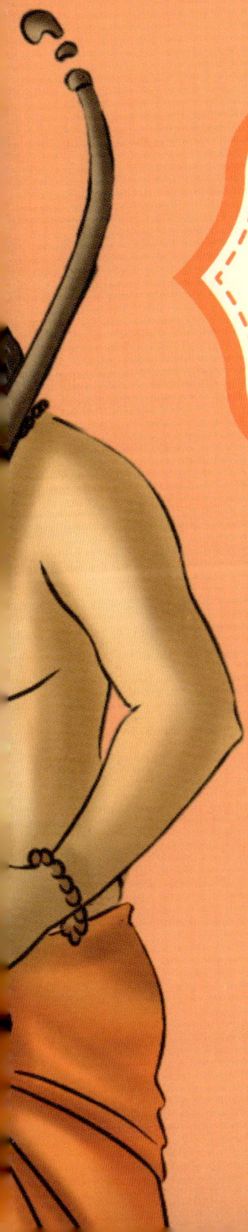

7

# Fill in the blanks to learn the tale of Sugriva and Bali's fight.

Sri Ram and Laxmana continued their relentless search for (a) __________. Following Kabandha's suggestions, they came to (b) ______________ to find and meet the exiled king (c) ________________ at the (d) _______________ mountain. Sugriva sent his best minister (e) ______________ to check on Rama and Laxmana as he doubted that they might be sent by his (f) brother ____________ to kill him.

The minister approached Rama and Laxman in the guise of a (g) ____________. In the first meeting itself Rama was very impressed with his use of (h) __________, his communication, and his intelligence. Similarly, the minister too saw the divinity in Sri Rama at the very first meeting. He then took Rama and Laxmana to meet Sugriva.

Rama and Sugriva were in similar situations when they met because both were exiled from their rightful places and faced the loss of loved ones. Rama and Sugriva got into a win-win agreement instantly. They agreed to help each other. Rama sent Sugriva to fight with Bali. Rama suggested that Sugriva wore a (i) ____________ for differentiation. Rama hid behind a tree and attacked the brother with a sharp arrow. He punished Bali for the sin he had committed by pushing his brother Sugriva out of his rightful kingdom and keeping Sugriva's wife (j) ____________ with him. The dying brother accepted his grave mistakes. Sugriva was crowned as the king, and his brother's son (k) ___________ was made the young prince.

After Sugriva became the king, he forgot his promise to Rama of finding Sita. When Laxmana reminded Sugriva of his promise and warned him of the consequences, Sugriva apologized and ordered his (l) ________ Sena (army) to start a massive search for Sita. While the army teams were preparing for their search, Rama entrusted his finger ring to Hanuman, knowing that it would help Sita recognize him. Rama had a divine intuition that Hanuman would be the one to successfully locate Sita, given his unmatched devotion and strength.

In the search for Mata Sita, Hanuman and (m) ____________ met (n) ___________, Jatayu's brother. Like his brother Jatayu, he too provided two crucial cues in the search for Mata Sita. The first was that she was kept inside Lanka by Ravana and that within Lanka, she was held in (o) ___________.

The wise Jambavan reminded Hanuman of his forgotten strengths. He called upon Hanuman and told him that he was born to accomplish the work of Sri Rama. Inspired by Jambavan's encouraging words, Hanuman prepared to leap across the ocean to find Sita and face any challenge that lay ahead in his quest.

# 8 Kishkinda Kanda Quiz

1. **How many sargas (chapters) are there in Kishkindha Kanda?**
   a) 57
   b) 67
   c) 81
   d) 60
2. **Who provided the crucial clue that Ravana had taken Mata Sita to Lanka across the sea?**
   a) Jatayu
   b) Kadambh
   c) Sampati
   d) Garuda
3. **What was the relationship between Sampati and Jatayu?**
   a) Father and son
   b) Friends
   c) Brothers
   d) Not related

4. **Where would the kingdom of Kishkindha be located in present-day India?**
   a) Uttar Pradesh
   b) Madhya Pradesh
   c) Tamil Naidu
   d) Karnataka

5. **In whose disguise did Hanuman come to meet Rama and Laxmana?**
   a) Saint
   b) Common man
   c) Vanar
   d) Demon

6. **Who is considered the father of Bali?**
   a) Indra Deva
   b) Surya Deva
   c) Brahma Deva
   d) Vayu Deva

7. **Who was Angada's mother?**
   a) Ruma
   b) Tara
   c) Rukmani
   d) Urmila

8. **During the exile, on which hill were Sugriva and his team residing?**
   a) Himalaya hill
   b) Aravali hill
   c) Rishimukha hill
   d) Mahendra hill

9. **In the presence of which element did Rama and Sugreeva become friends?**
   a) Air
   b) Water
   c) Fire
   d) Water

10. **To fight with which demon did Bali go inside a cave?**
   a) Dundubhi
   b) Mayavi
   c) Ravana
   d) Dooshan

11. **Who was Bali's wife?**
    a) Tara
    b) Menaka
    c) Mandodari
    d) Trijata
12. **Who was Sugriva's wife?**
    a) Ruma
    b) Menaka
    c) Mandodari
    d) Trijata
13. **Who was Bali's son?**
    a) Hanuman
    b) Angada
    c) Jambavan
    d) Naal
14. **Which sage's curse prevented Bali from fighting his brother Sugriva on the Rishimukha mountains?**
    a) Rishi Matanga
    b) Rishi Vashistha
    c) Rishi Bhardwaj
    d) Rishi Agusta
15. **Who reminded Hanuman of his forgotten powers?**
    a) Sugreeva
    b) Angad
    c) Jambavan
    d) Tara
16. **What object did Rama give Hanuman to help Sita recognize him as Rama's true messenger?**
    a) Handkerchief
    b) Garland
    c) Finger ring
    d) Flag
17. **What similarities did Rama and Sugriva share in their circumstances when they first met?**
    a) Both were cheated by their brothers.
    b) Both were away from their kingdom and their wives.
    c) Both were growing old.
    d) Both had a common enemy, Ravana.

**18. Over which mountain peak did Hanuman fly on the way to Lanka?**

a) Rishimukhya
b) Aravalli
c) Mainaka
d) Sursa

**19. How were Sugriva and Vali related?**

a) Brothers
b) Cousins
c) Friends
d) Rivals

**20. Which character is known for his immense strength but is killed by Rama in the Kishkindha Kanda?**

a) Hanuman
b) Bali
c) Sugriva
d) Kumbhakarna

**21. What event prompts Rama and Lakshmana to seek help from the *vanaras* in Kishkindha Kanda?**

a) The death of Vali
b) The abduction of Sita
c) The coronation of Sugriva
d) The alliance with Ravana

**22. On which hill did Rama and Laxmana wait for the rainy season to end in Kishkindha before resuming their search for Mata Sita?**

a) Himalaya hills
b) Aravalli hills
c) Mainaka hills
d) Rishimukha hills

**23. Who pacified Laxmana's anger when Sugriva forgot his promise to Rama?**

a) Tara
b) Ruma
c) Sita
d) Anjani

**24. Who wrote the *Hanuman Chalisa*?**

a) Rishi Valmiki
b) Kavi Kalidas
c) Acharya Tulsidas
d) Rishi Bhardwaj

25. **Who was Hanuman's father?**
   a) Kesari
   b) Indra
   c) Shiva
   d) Jambavan

26. **Who was Hanuman's mother?**
   a) Shakuntala
   b) Anjana
   c) Kruti
   d) Anasuya

27. **Which god blessed Mata Anjani and Kesari with a powerful and intelligent son, Hanuman?**
   a) Indra Deva
   b) Vishnu Deva
   c) Vayu Deva
   d) Agni Deva

28. **In which state of present-day India is Kishkindha located?**
   a) Tamil Naidu
   b) Andhra Pradesh
   c) Karnataka
   d) Madhya Pradesh

29. **Which quality of Hanumana impressed Rama the most?**
   a) His big and strong body
   b) His humbleness
   c) His intellect and great communication skills
   d) His friendship with Sugreeva

30. **What war cry did the monkey soldiers roar in their enthusiasm to defeat Ravana?**
   a) Sugriiva *aaj na*—the inviolable order of Sugreeva
   b) Jai Shree Ram
   c) Jai Hanuman
   d) Om

31. **In which direction did Sugreeva send his strongest team for the search of Mata Sita?**
   a) North
   b) South
   c) East
   d) West

**32. Hanuman was part of which expedition team sent to search for Mata Sita?**

a) North
b) South
c) East
d) West

**33. Until what point did Sugreeva instruct the northern expedition team to search for Mata Sita?**

a) Udaya Mountain
b) Mahendra Mountains
c) Astamana Mountain
d) Somagiri Mountain

**34. Until what point did Sugreeva instruct the western expedition team to search for Mata Sita?**

a) Udaya Mountain
b) Mahendra Mountains
c) Astagiri Mountain
d) Somagiri Mountain

**35. Until what point did Sugreeva instruct the eastern expedition team to search for Mata Sita?**

a) Udaya Mountain
b) Mahendra Mountains
c) Astamana Mountain
d) Somagiri Mountain

**36. From which mountain did Hanuman take off for Lanka in his search for Mata Sita?**

a) Udaya Mountain
b) Mahendra Mountains
c) Astamana Mountain
d) Sonagiri Mountain

**37. In which language did Lord Hanuman communicate with Rama during their first interaction?**

a) Hindi
b) Kannada
c) Awadhi
d) Sanskrit

**38. What promise did Sugriva make to Rama after Bali's defeat?**

a) To always be loyal to Rama
b) To help find Sita
c) To join Rama in the battle against Ravana
d) To provide Rama with an army of vanaras

**39. Why did Hanuman carry Rama's ring with him to Lanka?**

a) It gave Hanuman the power to fly.
b) It would have helped Hanuman earn Mata Sita's trust.
c) It was Rama's gift to Hanuman.
d) Hanuman thought it would give him luck.

**40. In the Mahabharata, whose chariot's flag bore the image of Hanuman?**

a) Yudhistira
b) Bheem
c) Arjun
d) Nakul

# NAME THESE 2 RAMAYANA CHARACTERS

Check answers on page 148

Explore the Story of

# Sundar Kanda

## 9

# Fill in the blanks to learn the tale of Bhagwan Hanuman's successful search for Mata Sita.

Motivated by the words of ______________ (a), Hanuman finally remembered his extraordinary powers. Hanuman took off for Lanka in the search of Mata Sita. The ocean was enormous. Hanuman jumped, swam, and leaped to cross the ocean. On the way, he was obstructed and tested by ___________ (b) and ___________ (c) for his power, intellect, and presence of mind. With his wit, agility, and commitment for Rama's task, Hanuman outsmarted both of them. Overcoming many such obstructions and hindrances, he finally reached Lanka. He was awestruck on seeing the beautiful, magnificent, golden city of Lanka, designed by none other than the master architect ________________ (d). Hanuman also observed that Lanka was heavily guarded by demons.

Hanuman eliminated _______________ (e) to enter Lanka. Now, the next task was to trace ______________ (f). Hanuman tirelessly searched street by street for Sita, encountering many women but finding none who matched her grace. To re-energize himself, Hanuman ventured into a garden and spotted a lady sitting quietly. Her grace and aura resonated with Rama's description of Sita, prompting him to hide behind a nearby tree to observe her closely.

Then Hanuman observed ______________ (g) approaching Sita, demanding her to marry him. Sita boldly refused and warned him of dire consequences for keeping her captive. Rattled by her defiance, Ravana gave her an ultimatum - marry him or face death in two months. Hanuman sang ______________ (h) from the tree, capturing Sita's attention and bringing her the news of Rama's well-being. While she wanted to trust him, her past experience with Ravana made her cautious about misjudging once again.

Sita asked Hanuman to prove his identity, fearing he might be a demon, so he showed her Rama's ____________ (i), which brought her to tears. To ensure Rama would believe him, Sita gave Hanuman her ____________ (j) as a counter passcode.

Hanuman accomplished a key milestone by finding Sita. Now he wanted to gather intelligence about Lanka and Ravana. So, he created chaos in the ____________ (k), prompting Ravana to send armies that were swiftly defeated. Ravana's son ____________ (l) was killed by Hanuman in this encounter. Finally, Ravana's other son ____________ (m) recognized Hanuman's extraordinary strength and used the ultimate option, ____________ (n) to capture him, which Hanuman accepted willingly.

At Ravana's court, Hanuman declared himself as Rama's messenger and urged Ravana to seek forgiveness and return Sita to avoid destruction. Enraged, Ravana ordered Hanuman's capture, but his brother ____________ (o) reminded the court that killing a messenger was against their laws. So, Ravana had Hanuman's __________ (p) set on fire, but thanks to Sita's prayer, Hanuman was unharmed.

Using his flaming tail as a torch, he set fire to nearly __________ (q) of Lanka while assessing its strengths and weaknesses alongside. This act warned Ravana and his army that if one messenger could cause such chaos, they should fear the destruction that Rama's entire force could unleash.

# 10 Sundar Kanda Quiz

1. **What was Hanuman's main weapon?**
   a) Sword
   b) Trident
   c) Mace
   d) Spear

2. **Who was Hanuman's guru?**
   a) Sun
   b) Sugreeva
   c) Vishnu
   d) Jambavan

3. **In what form did Hanuman meet Rama and Laxmana for the very first time?**
   a) Sage
   b) Common man
   c) King
   d) Monkey

4. **Who advised Hanuman to serve Bali and Sugriva in Kishkindha?**
   a) His mother, Anjana
   b) His father, Kesari
   c) Bhagwan Vishnu
   d) Bhagwan Shiva

5. **Which city is known as the birthplace of Hanuman? In which Indian state is it located?**
   a) Panchvati, Maharashtra
   b) Chitrakoot, Uttar Pradesh
   c) Hampi, Karnataka
   d) Rameshwaram, Tamil Nadu

6. **Who convinced Hanuman that he could easily cross over the ocean to reach Lanka?**
   a) Sugriva
   b) Angad

c) Rama
d) Jambavan

**7. Where did Hanuman meet Mata Sita in Lanka?**

a) Lanka Palace
b) Ashok Vatika
c) Mandodari Palace
d) Dandaka Jungle

**8. What piece of jewellery did Mata Sita give to Hanuman as a unique identifier to show to Bhagwan Rama?**

a) Earring
b) Finger ring
c) Bangle
d) Crest jewel

**9. Whose prayers protected Hanuman from the fire lit by Ravana's army on his tail?**

a) Mata Sita
b) Vibhishan
c) Ravan
d) Ruma

**10. How many *chaupais* are there in the Hanuman Chalisa?**

a) 20
b) 40
c) 50
d) 30

**11. Which mountain obstructed Hanuman as he was crossing the sea to Lanka?**

a) Mandar
b) Mainaka
c) Mahendra
d) Rishimukh

**12. Which demon serpent tried to block Hanuman's path as he leaped to Lanka?**

a) Surasa
b) Lankini
c) Tadaka
d) Tara

**13. Who tried to stop Hanuman from entering Lanka?**

a) Lankini
b) Sulochana
c) Mandodari
d) Trijata

**14. Which demon urged Ravana to return Sita to Rama?**

a) Indrajeet
b) Akshay Kumar
c) Vibhishan
d) Prahasta

**15. What did Hanuman observe in Lanka while searching for Mata Sita?**

a) People playing the game of chess
b) Vedic hymns being sung
c) That the city of Lanka was heavily guarded
d) All of the above

**16. How did Hanuman signal to Mata Sita from atop a tree that he was Rama's messenger?**

a) By throwing a fruit at her
b) By singing the story of Rama
c) By making monkey noises
d) By jumping in front of Mata Sita

**17. On which mountain did Hanuman sit to assess the entire city of Lanka after reaching there?**

a) Chitrakoot Mountain
b) Himalaya Mountain

c) Trikuta Mountain
d) Mahendra Mountain

**18. Which is the famous line from the Hanuman Chalisa indicating Hanuman's ability to dispel negativity?**
a) *Ram bhajan karat jinh...*
b) *Bhoot pishach nikat nahi aave...*
c) *Sankat se Hanuman chhudave...*
d) *Pavan tanay sankat haran...*

**19. Which son of Ravana did Hanuman kill at Ashoka Vatika in Lanka?**
a) Indrajeet
b) Meghnad
c) Akshay Kumar
d) Vibhishan

**20. What was Hanuman doing while simultaneously setting fire to Lanka?**
a) Killing as many demons as he could
b) Shaming as many demons as he could
c) Assessing the strengths, weaknesses, and fortification of Lanka
d) Stealing wealth from Lanka

**21. To which arrow did Hanuman willingly surrender and allow himself to be captured?**
a) Indrajeet's Brahmastra
b) Ravan's Pashupatastra
c) Indrajeet's Nagastra
d) Ravana's Brahmastra

**22. Which of the following demons did Hanuman kill on the battlefield of Lanka?**
a) Indrajit
b) Kumbhakarna
c) Ravana
d) Nikumbha

**23. What best describes Hanuman?**
a) Demon
b) Deity
c) An ardent devotee of Rama
d) King

**24. In the Mahabharat, which Pandava was unable to lift Hanuman's tail that was blocking his way?**

a) Sahadeva
b) Nakul
c) Bheem
d) Yudhisther

**25. Under the custody of which Mughal emperor did Acharya Tulsidas write Hanuman Chalisa?**

a) Akbar
b) Shah Jahan
c) Aurangzeb
d) Babar

**26. Which phrase in the Hanuman Chalisa expresses Hanuman's loyalty to Rama?**

a) *Bajrang bali*
b) *Rama doot*
c) *Sankat se Hanuman chhudave*
d) *Dukh dard haro*

**27. Who was the architect of Lanka?**

a) Ravana
b) Meghnad
c) Vishwakarma
d) Vibhishan

**28. What did Hanuman say to motivate Sita?**

a) That Rama will come soon to save her.
b) That she should give up hope now.
c) That he will get good food for her.
d) That he will kill Ravana.

**29. What did Hanuman do after speaking to Sita?**

a) Fight Ravana
b) Start creating havoc at Ashoka Vatika
c) Celebrate in Lanka
d) Take Sita away

**30. Which of the following is not a name for Bhagwan Hanuman?**

a) Anjaneya
b) Maruti
c) Vayuputra
d) Indrajeet

31. **How did Hanuman manage to burn Lanka?**
   a) By using a magical weapon
   b) By setting his tail on fire
   c) By invoking a spell
   d) By causing an earthquake

32. **Whom did Hanuman see in Ravana's court, speaking about dharma and praising Rama?**
   a) Indrajeet
   b) Meghnad
   c) Akshay Kumar
   d) Vibhishan

33. **What kind of city does Hanuman find on reaching Lanka?**
   a) Beautiful and prosperous
   b) Ruined and desolate
   c) Small and insignificant
   d) Large but dilapidated

34. **Hanuman Chalisa has 40 *chaupais*. How many *dohas* does it have?**
   a) 43
   b) 3
   c) 10
   d) 40

35. **Whose incarnation was Laxmana?**
   a) Vishnu
   b) Shiva
   c) Sheshnag
   d) Surya Dev

36. **Using his two powers of becoming small and big, Hanuman defeated Surasa. They are called Mahima and ____________.**
   a) Isitva
   b) Prapti
   c) Garima
   d) Anima

37. **When Ravana heard Hanuman's proposal of truce, asking for forgiveness from Rama and the return of Sita, how did Ravana respond?**
   a) Ravana considered the proposal.
   b) Ravana agreed to the proposal.
   c) Ravana asked his soldiers to kill Hanuman.
   d) Ravana left his courtroom.

**38. Who is the main protagonist in Sundara Kanda?**

a) Ravana
b) Hanuman
c) Laxmana
d) Sita

**39. How does Sundara Kanda conclude?**

a) With Ravana's defeat
b) With Sita's rescue
c) With Hanuman's return to Rama
d) With a celebration in Lanka

**40. Who shared her dream about Rama triumphing over Ravana?**

a) Sita
b) Mandodari
c) Kaikeyi
d) Trijata

Explore
Yu
Ka

Story of
ha
da

# 11 Fill in the blanks to learn about the epic battle between Rama and Ravana.

(a) ______________ returned victorious from Lanka, leaving it in ruins and Ravana furious. (b) _____________ advised Ravana to return Sita and avoid war, condemning the immorality of his actions. Unmoved, Ravana dismissed the suggestion, questioning his brother's loyalty and forcing him to leave. Previously, (c) ____________ had warned Ravana against kidnapping Sita, recounting his encounters with Rama and Lakshmana. (d) ______________, (e) ______________, and (f) ______________ also urged Ravana to reconsider, but he ignored their pleas. Instead, Ravana surrounded himself with war-hungry yes-men who boosted his ego and solidified his resolve for conflict.

Ousted from (g) ___________, Ravana's brother faced a dilemma: should he leave Ravana and join Rama? He approached (h) ____________, seeking to stand with him in the war, viewing Rama as the embodiment of dharma. Rama hesitated, consulting his team, which had mixed opinions. (i) _____________ and the others feared Vibhishana might be a spy for Ravana, while (j) ______________ supported Vibhishana, citing his integrity for dharma. Aware of the need for local knowledge of Ravana's strategies and Lanka's geography, Rama ultimately accepted Vibhishana into his team.

Now Rama faced the daunting challenge of crossing the (k) ___________ to reach Lanka. Initially praying to the sea for assistance, he realized that mere patience was insufficient for any negotiation. Recognizing the need for strength, he prepared to dry up the ocean with his (l) ____________, prompting the Sea God to appear. The Sea God advised constructing a bridge, with the help of (m) _____________ and (n) ___________. This moment highlights the importance of determination, collaboration, and balance between diplomacy and strength.

The (o) ____________ was constructed enabling the Vanara Sena to reach Lanka. Rama, having sharpened his war skills during his exile, strategically positioned his forces at the (p) __________ gates of Lanka. Rama wanted to avoid the war. So, he sent (q) _____________ to convince Ravana for a truce but the efforts failed. The battle erupted, with (r) ____________ wounding Rama and Laxmana with his serpent arrows. Rescued by Garuda, Rama's forces retaliated, inflicting heavy losses on Ravana's army. With Ravana's brother (s) ___________ and his son Indrajit as the last formidable warriors on Ravana's side, the conflict intensified. (t) _________ eliminated Kumbhkaran. Indrajit came to the battlefield with a determination to end the war. His vigorous attacks made Rama, Laxmana, and a large part of the (u) ___________ army fall unconscious. Hanuman was sent to fetch vital (v) ____________ herbs from the Himalayas. Unable to identify the required herb, he uprooted an entire mountain and returned, healing Rama, Laxmana, and his army. Once revived, Laxmana eliminated Indrajit without any delay.

Now the universe was waiting for the intense battle between Rama and Ravana. Despite Ravana's powers and intellect, Rama, guided by his able charioteer Matali, ultimately defeated him using the (w) ____________. Rather than claiming Lanka, Rama made (x) _____________ the king of Lanka. The celebration of (y) _____________ commemorates this victory of good over evil. Rama and the whole team return to Ayodhya with Mata Sita. Rama was coronated as the King of Ayodhya, and we all celebrate (z) ____________ to mark Rama's return after 14 years of exile.

# 12 Yudha Kanda Quiz

1. **Who led the construction of Ram Setu?**
   a) Angad
   b) Sugreev
   c) Nala
   d) Jambavan
2. **How long was the Ram Setu?**
   a) 30 miles
   b) 100 miles
   c) 200 miles
   d) 10 miles
3. **Who wrote the lyrics for the renowned Shiv Tandav Stotram?**
   a) Vishnu
   b) Ravana
   c) Tansen
   d) Shiva
4. **In which yuga did the story of Ramayana unfold?**
   a) Treta Yuga
   b) Dwapar Yuga
   c) Kali Yuga
   d) Saat Yuga
5. **Which of the following demons urged Ravana to return Sita to Rama?**
   a) Indrajeet
   b) Akshay Kumar
   c) Vibhishan
   d) Prahasta
6. **Ravana is traditionally depicted as having how many heads?**
   a) 12
   b) 100
   c) 101
   d) 10

**7. Who was the commander-in-chief of Ravana's army?**

a) Prahasta
b) Indrajeet
c) Kumbhkaran
d) Malayvan

**8. Who was the king of Lanka prior to Ravana?**

a) Malyavan
b) Kuber
c) Bali
d) Kesari

**9. Who was another one of Ravana's wife, besides Mandodari?**

a) Urvashi
b) Menaka
c) Dhanyamalini
d) Kritika

**10. How many sons did Ravana have from his three wives?**

a) Four
b) Five
c) Six
d) Seven

**11. Which mountain from the Himalayas did Hanuman lift and bring to Lanka to save the lives of Rama, Laxmana, and the Vanara army?**

a) Nilgiri
b) Dronagiri
c) Kailash
d) Nanda Parvat

**12. Who were the two informers of Ravana who disguised themselves as Vanaras to infliltrate Rama's army?**

a) Atikaya and Devantaka
b) Narantaka and Trishriras
c) Akampa and Parhasta
d) Shuka and Sarana

**13. Which demoness revealed the truth to the grieving Sita when she saw the illusory severed head of Rama?**

a) Trijata
b) Mandodari
c) Lankini
d) Dhanyamalini

**14. How was Malyavan related to Ravana?**

a) Paternal grandfather
b) Maternal grandfather
c) Father
d) Cousin brother

**15. Who killed the demons Rashmiketu and Agniketu?**

a) Rama
b) Sugreeva
c) Laxmana
d) Nala

**16. Who killed Kumbhakarna's son Nikumbh?**

a) Rama
b) Sugreeva
c) Lakshman
d) Hanuman

**17. Which demon rendered Rama and Laxmana unconscious by a serpent arrow?**

a) Indrajeet
b) Rashmiketu
c) Nikumbh
d) Ravana

**18. Who killed the demon Akampan?**

a) Rama
b) Sugreeva
c) Hanuman
d) Lakshman

**19. Name the serpent weapon Indrajeet used against Rama and Laxmana.**

a) Brahmastra
b) Nagpash
c) Pinaak dhanush
d) Vajra

**20. Who cursed Kumbhakarna to sleep continuously for six months?**

a) Goddess Durga
b) Goddess Saraswati
c) Sage Durvasa
d) Bhagwan Brahma

**21. Who killed Kumbhakarna?**

a) Rama
b) Sugreeva
c) Hanuman
d) Laxmana

**22. Who killed Ravana's brave son Devantaka?**

a) Rama
b) Sugreeva
c) Hanuman
d) Laxmana

**23. Which herb did Hanuman bring from the Himalayas to revive Rama and Laxmana?**

a) Sanjeevani
b) Basil
c) Ashwagandha
d) Shatavari

**24. Who killed Meghnad?**

a) Laxmana
b) Rama
c) Hanuman
d) Angad

**25. What was the name of the famous aerial plane used by Ravana?**

a) Agni Vimana
b) Shakuna Vimana
c) Pushpaka Vimana
d) Dhanush Vimana

**26. Who prevented Ravana from beheading Sita when he tried to kill her in a fit of rage?**

a) Trijata
b) Mandodari
c) Kekasi
d) Dhanyamalini

**27. What symbol adorned the flag on Ravana's chariot?**

a) Trident
b) Bow and arrow
c) Veena
d) Sword

**28. Which weapon did Rama use to kill Ravana?**

a) Mace
b) Chakra
c) Sword
d) Arrow

**29. Hanuman killed the youngest son of Ravana when he visited Lanka for the first time. Who was he?**

a) Atikaya
b) Akshaya Kumar
c) Indrajit
d) Meghnad

**30. Who killed Ravana's most powerful and beloved son Indrajit?**

a) Laxmana
b) Rama
c) Hanuman
d) Angad

**31. Who killed Prahasta, the chief commander of Ravana's army?**

a) Angad
b) Nala
c) Neel
d) Laxmana

**32. Who killed the demon Khara?**

a) Rama
b) Laxmana
c) Hanuman
d) Bharata

**33. Who was the first demon or demoness killed by Rama?**

a) Mareech
b) Subhau
c) Khar
d) Tadaka

**34. Whom did Rama kill to get Sugreeva his kingdom and wife back?**

a) Khara
b) Meghnad
c) Bali
d) Atikaya

**35. Apart from Ravana, which other warrior did Rama kill in the battle at Lanka?**

a) Indrajit
b) Kumbhakaran
c) Akshay
d) Lankini

**36. What was the name of the vaidya (doctor) who healed Laxmana and Rama after Indrajit's attack, using the herbs brought by Hanuman?**

a) Rishi Agastya
b) Sushen
c) Jatayu
d) Rishi Atri

**37. Who were Ravana's parents?**

a) Rishi Vashisth and Mata Arundhati
b) Rishi Rishyasringa and Mata Shanta
c) Rishi Bharadwaj and Mata Shusheela
d) Rishi Visharva and Mata Kaikesi

**38. Who provided Rama with a chariot during the final battle against Ravana?**

a) Agni
a) Brahma
b) Indra
c) Vishnu

**39. Who performed the funeral rites for Ravana?**

a) Vibhishana
b) Hanuman
c) Rama
d) Sugreeva

**40. Whom did Rama declare as the future king of Lanka after eliminating Ravana?**

a) Laxamana
b) Hanuman
c) Vibhishan
d) Jambavan

# NAME THESE 6 RAMAYANA CHARACTERS

1. 
2. 
3. 
4. 
5. 
6. 

Check answers on page 148

# B

# Brain Teasers on Ramayana

# 13

# Sequence the Story

**Arrange the following events from the Ramayana in the correct order.**

1. **a) Four princes of Ayodhya got married to the four princesses of Mithila.**
   **b) Rama killed the demoness Tadka.**
   **c) King Dashratha went to Rishi Rishyasringa barefoot.**
   **d) Rama, Bharat, Laxmana, and Shatrughan were born.**

   a) d, c, b, a
   b) c, d, b, a
   c) c, d, a, b
   d) d, c, a, b

2. **a) Kaikeyi asks Dashratha for her two boons.**
   **b) Parshuram arrives in the court of King Janak.**
   **c) Rama breaks Shiva's bow.**
   **d) Manthara successfully poisons Kaikeyi's mind.**

   a) c, b, a, d
   b) c, a, b, d
   c) a, b, d, c
   d) c, b, d, a

3. **a) Rama breaks Shiva's bow.**
   **b) Kaikeyi gifts Kanaka Bhavan to Rama and Sita.**
   **c) Parshuram arrives in the court of King Janak.**
   **d) Rama kills Tadaka.**

   a) c, a, b, d
   b) c, d, a, b
   c) b, d, a, c
   d) d, a, c, b

4. **a) Rishi Vishwamitra comes to Ayodhya and takes Rama and Laxaman with him.**
   **b) Rama marries Mata Sita.**
   **c) Rama kills Tadaka.**
   **d) Rama freed Mata Ahalya from her curse.**

a) a, b, c, d
b) a, c, d, b
c) a, b, d, c
d) a, d, c, b

5. **a) Rama, Sita, and Laxmana settle in Chitrakoot.**
   **b) Bharatha meets Rama at Chitrakoot.**
   **c) Rama hugs Guha.**
   **d) Rama, Sita, and Laxmana begin their exile from Ayodhya.**

   a) d, a, b, c
   b) d, b, a, c
   c) d, c, a, b
   d) d, b, c, a

6. **a) Rama departs for the forest.**
   **b) Bharatha decides to bring Rama back.**
   **c) Bharatha places Rama's sandals on Ayodhya's throne.**
   **d) Rishi Bhardwaj guides Bharatha about Rama's whereabouts.**

   a) a, b, d, c
   b) a, d, c, b
   c) a, c, d, b
   d) a, b, c, d

7. **a) Rama decides to leave Chitrakoot.**
   **b) Rama and Bharatha meet in Chitrakoot.**
   **c) Rishi Bhardwaj advises Bharatha to go to Chitrakoot.**
   **d) Rishi Bhardwaj advises Rama to go to Chitrakoot.**

   a) d, c, b, a
   b) b, c, d, a
   c) b, a, c, d
   d) b, a, d, c

8. **a) Rama and Laxaman fight with Khara and Dushana.**
   **b) Laxmana cuts Surpanakha's nose and ears.**
   **c) Mareech turns into a golden deer.**
   **d) Surpanakha asks Rama to marry her.**

   a) d, c, b, a
   b) b, c, d, a
   c) d, b, a, c
   d) b, a, d, c

9. a) **Mareech advises Ravana not to abduct Mata Sita.**
   b) **Mareech turns into a golden deer.**
   c) **Laxaman asks Mata Sita not to cross the line drawn outside the hut.**
   d) **Ravana appears as a sage in front of Mata Sita.**

   a) d, c, b, a
   b) a, b, c, d
   c) b, a, c, d
   d) a, b, d, c

10. a) **Laxmana attacks Surpanakha.**
    b) **Rama and Laxman fight with Kabandha.**
    c) **Rama kills Bali.**
    d) **Rama kills Tadaka.**

    a) d, a, b, c
    b) a, b, c, d
    c) b, a, c, d
    d) d, b, a, c

11. a) **Ravana abducts Sita.**
    b) **Ravana takes Mata Sita to Ashok Vatika in Lanka.**
    c) **Sita gets a shock and falls unconscious at the sight of Rama's cut head and bow.**
    d) **Sita asks Hanuman to describe Rama's various characteristics.**

    a) d, a, b, c
    b) a, b, c, d
    c) b, a, c, d
    d) a, b, d, c

12. a) **Hanuman consoles Tara on the death of Bali.**
    b) **Hanuman meets Rama and Laxmana in a sanyasi's disguise.**
    c) **Hanuman goes to Lanka in search of Mata Sita.**
    d) **Hanuman reminds Sugreeva to fulfil his promise to Rama.**

    a) d, a, b, c
    b) b, a, c, d
    c) b, a, d, c
    d) a, b, d, c

13. a) **Sugreeva sends Vanaras to search for Mata Sita.**
    b) **Hanuman goes across the sea to Lanka.**
    c) **Sugreeva is crowned the king of Kishkindha.**
    d) **Sampati hears of Jatayu's death.**

a) c, a, d, b
b) b, a, c, d
c) b, a, d, c
d) c, b, d, a

**14. a) Sugreeva apologizes to Laxmana for missing his promise.**
**b) Hanuman, Tara, Angad, and Janmbvan reach the seashore.**
**c) Vanara Sena is sent to all four directions in search of Mata Sita.**
**d) Jambavan motivates Hanumana to recall his powers.**

a) c, a, d, b
b) a, c, b, d
c) a, b, d, c
d) c, b, d, a

**15. a) Hanuman starts his search for Mata Sita at Ashoka Vatika.**
**b) Hanuman kills Ravana's son Akshay Kumar.**
**c) Hanuman returns to Rama with Sita's chudamani.**
**d) Hanuman narrates the story of Rama to Mata Sita.**

a) c, a, d, b
b) a, c, b, d
c) a, d, b, c
d) c, b, d, a

**16. a) Rama visits the ashram of Rishi Agastya.**
**b) Rama meets the injured Jatayu.**
**c) Rama defeats demons Khara and Dushana along with their armies.**
**d) Rama releases demon Kabandha from a curse.**

a) c, a, d, b
b) a, c, b, d
c) a, d, b, c
d) c, b, d, a

**17. a) Rama requests Sea God to show him the way.**
**b) Rama reaches the Rishyamukha mountain to meet Sugreeva.**
**c) Rama promises Sugreeva that he would get back his kingdom.**
**d) Rama kills Kumbhakaran.**

a) b, a, c, b
b) a, c, b, d
c) a, d, b, c
d) b, c, a, d

18. **a) Ravana orders his soldiers to kill Hanuman.**
    **b) Indrajeet uses the brahmastra to capture Hanuman.**
    **c) Hanuman burns Lanka.**
    **d) Vibhishana favours Hanuman in Ravana's court.**

    a) b, a, d, c
    b) a, c, b, d
    c) a, b, c, d
    d) b, c, a, d

19. **a) Laxmana kills Indrajeet.**
    **b) Rama kills Ravana.**
    **c) Angada tries for a truce one last time.**
    **d) Vibhishana becomes the king of Lanka.**

    a) b, a, d, c
    b) a, c, b, d
    c) c, b, a, d
    d) c, a, b, d

20. **a) Rama kills Khar and Dushan.**
    **b) Rama kills Ravana.**
    **c) Rama kills Tadaka.**
    **d) Vishnu takes an avatar in the form of Rama to destroy demons on earth.**

    a) b, c, a, d
    b) a, c, b, d
    c) c, b, a, d
    d) d, c, a, b

# MAZES



Help Hanuman find his way to Mata Sita.

Maze #2

Imagine Laxmana went out to fetch fresh fruits and vegetables. While returning, he lost his way back to the hut. Help Laxmana to trace his path.

# Maze #3

Young Rama and Laxmana while living in the forest with Rishi Vishwamitra collected firewood for cooking. One day, they lost their way home. Help them find the correct route to the ashram before sunset.

# Maze #4

Laxmana went deep into the forest in the search of sweet fruits for Rama and Sita. Help him return quickly.

# Maze #5

Help little Hanuman find his way back to his mother Anjani.

# Maze #6

Bharata reached Rishi Bhardwaj's ashram while looking for Rama. The rishi directs him to go to Chitrakoot. Which path should Bharata take to reach Rama?

## Maze #7

Imagine you are a bird observing Mata Sita collect firewood in the forest. Help her find her way back to the hut.

# Maze #8

Rama, Lakshmana, and Sita are on their way to Rishi Agastya's ashram. Help them reach quickly.

# Maze #9

The Vanar Sena has lost its way
in the search for Mata Sita.
Can you guide them in
the right direction?

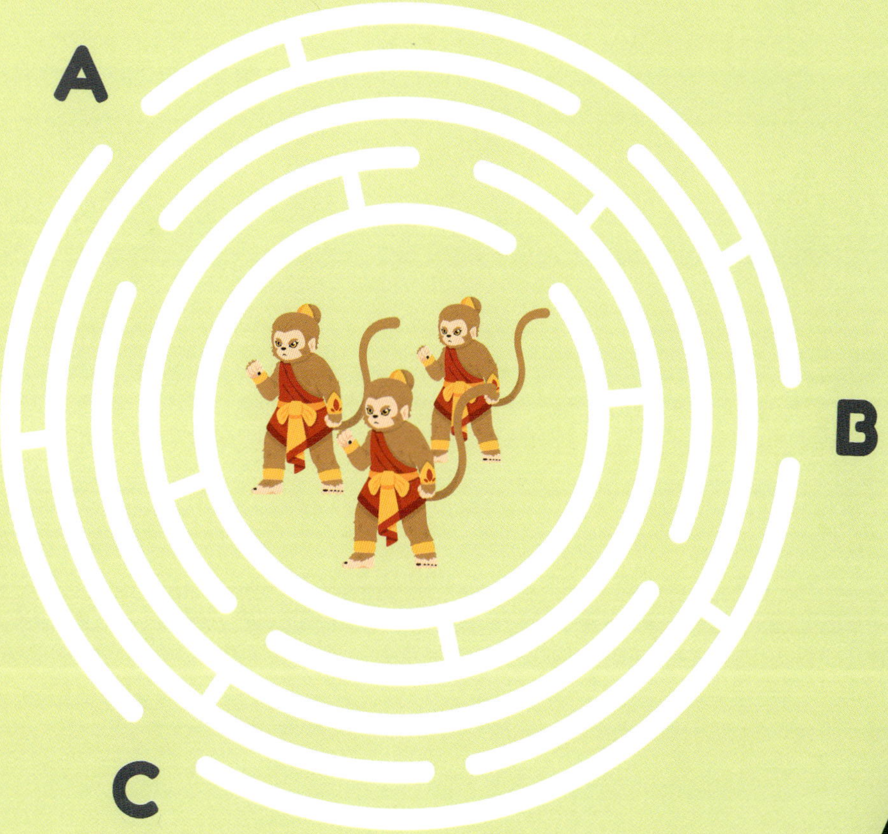

# Maze #10

Hanuman is trying to enter Lanka. Help him navigate through the streets of Lanka.

# Maze #11

Help Rama reach Mata Sita.

# 15

## Word Search #1

Find the 5 leadership qualities of Rama hidden in the word maze below.

| X | Z | Q | T | G | U | U | R | O | E | Z | T | R | S | Q | R | A | O |
|---|---|---|---|---|---|---|---|---|---|---|---|---|---|---|---|---|---|
| I | L | M | O | L | H | A | P | E | J | J | Z | T | X | G | N | W | T |
| U | J | C | F | K | R | X | T | Q | S | D | L | R | Z | Q | X | N | X |
| A | Q | H | F | F | H | K | B | U | W | P | B | G | R | F | I | C | Y |
| W | P | Q | C | V | Q | Z | A | O | W | H | O | E | S | N | P | Q | D |
| H | Z | A | I | K | R | N | J | T | Q | L | Z | N | Y | O | H | D | L |
| O | L | O | R | J | V | F | I | U | K | D | U | F | S | T | R | V | X |
| N | B | O | B | E | D | I | E | N | T | V | E | G | K | I | Y | K | R |
| E | A | S | O | Y | T | Z | V | N | R | Z | T | Z | I | N | B | K | R |
| S | U | S | E | H | I | Z | H | L | Q | Q | I | U | N | Q | X | L | I |
| T | X | K | B | N | U | G | A | I | A | B | N | T | D | Q | W | R | E |
| R | O | T | R | U | T | H | F | U | L | G | C | S | H | G | E | S | E |

**HINT**

TRUTHFUL | HONEST | RESPONSIBLE | KIND | OBEDIENT

# Word Search #2

Spot the 9 characters from the Ramayana hidden in the word maze below.

| | | | | | | | | | | | | | | | | | |
|---|---|---|---|---|---|---|---|---|---|---|---|---|---|---|---|---|---|
| Q | F | S | H | A | B | A | R | I | T | A | N | P | D | G | U | G | V |
| F | D | D | B | J | G | I | B | Y | X | A | Z | U | H | Q | F | X | V |
| A | F | R | J | X | H | C | H | D | Z | U | B | K | P | Q | Z | K | Q |
| F | G | R | A | Z | T | L | S | U | G | R | E | E | V | A | K | A | I |
| Z | Q | H | I | M | J | H | S | C | R | E | T | L | L | V | E | F | J |
| M | K | A | T | M | A | K | I | S | H | K | I | N | D | A | I | T | S |
| Q | H | N | V | W | M | F | D | F | I | Y | J | L | Y | U | B | O | U |
| L | O | U | V | I | B | H | E | E | S | H | A | N | A | Y | T | U | T |
| M | L | M | C | H | D | C | R | A | Y | O | D | H | Y | A | Q | D | L |
| G | V | A | L | A | K | S | H | M | A | N | A | J | L | H | H | B | T |
| U | L | N | S | H | K | C | F | U | D | N | V | B | W | W | F | U | I |
| R | X | X | A | K | E | V | A | T | H | Q | K | F | D | R | W | R | P |

**HINT**

RAMA | KEVAT | LAKSHMANA | SHABARI | HANUMAN

KISHKINDA | VIBHEESHANA | SUGREEVA

# Word Search #3

Find out the 5 different names of Mata Sita hidden in the word maze below.

| | | | | | | | | | | | | | | | | | |
|---|---|---|---|---|---|---|---|---|---|---|---|---|---|---|---|---|---|
| A | A | E | P | Z | L | D | B | J | Q | H | H | S | D | V | S | T | T |
| J | A | N | K | I | Y | N | H | C | D | J | D | I | C | F | U | K | D |
| S | R | E | F | U | J | I | O | N | Y | V | B | X | N | L | I | V | A |
| I | V | J | E | K | S | T | O | R | C | Y | O | G | L | X | K | K | X |
| H | A | Y | B | U | E | F | M | W | W | P | E | B | Z | X | F | X | W |
| C | I | P | X | H | E | Q | I | W | R | O | U | O | F | G | B | B | Y |
| T | D | N | O | T | U | V | K | L | I | I | V | P | G | N | N | V | V |
| N | H | F | T | Y | N | M | M | A | I | T | H | I | L | I | A | O | G |
| N | E | Z | Z | Q | S | N | I | K | P | G | T | Y | O | U | D | N | X |
| G | Z | B | J | X | W | P | R | J | Y | A | S | P | R | Y | E | D | K |
| S | I | D | X | A | V | O | Y | A | A | E | Z | H | I | Z | M | K | C |
| D | D | X | T | J | L | R | L | Y | Y | X | L | M | D | G | O | L | W |

**HINT**

BHOOMI | JANKI | VAIDHE | MAITHILI | BHUMIJA

# Word Search #4

Hanuman inspires us to be better humans.
Can you find the 5 qualities of Hanuman
that we should adopt in our lives?

| Z | R | R | R | K | R | E | B | K | L | F | I | Z | Q | S | U | V | B |
|---|---|---|---|---|---|---|---|---|---|---|---|---|---|---|---|---|---|
| H | T | W | U | L | G | E | K | O | S | W | I | S | E | P | H | W | R |
| J | A | N | R | R | K | H | B | O | S | O | E | V | L | Q | J | L | A |
| E | A | J | G | H | R | G | H | I | T | Z | C | B | B | D | O | H | V |
| S | T | O | V | M | D | G | D | S | R | H | F | E | W | W | U | U | E |
| G | W | J | L | X | I | J | X | L | E | P | F | H | D | N | Y | M | Q |
| X | M | V | R | D | R | L | Y | I | N | S | F | R | Q | F | G | I | S |
| K | N | X | J | S | T | Q | P | L | G | D | E | D | C | N | E | L | E |
| S | C | B | U | K | Q | R |  | O | T | H | C | Q | W | D | W | I | U |
| W | R | S | E | M | A | U | W | R | H | R | U | P | B | O | X | T | N |
| D | Q | S | F | W | V | F | L | O | Y | A | L | T | Y | F | W | Y | V |
| G | R | P | F | P | V | X | L | W | G | C | Z | V | B | A | A | C | C |

**HINT**

STRENGTH | HUMILITY | WISE | LOYAL | BRAVE

# Word Search #5

Mata Sita is an inspiration for everyone.
Can you find the 5 qualities of Mata Sita in the word maze below.

| | | | | | | | | | | | | | | | | | |
|---|---|---|---|---|---|---|---|---|---|---|---|---|---|---|---|---|---|
| G | R | O | A | F | G | X | V | V | G | W | B | T | W | W | E | B | L |
| R | O | I | X | P | O | W | E | R | F | U | L | O | P | N | B | Q | D |
| R | D | D | K | Q | B | P | X | F | X | P | V | L | M | K | R | G | W |
| Z | X | Y | F | O | I | J | K | E | C | V | A | E | B | E | E | F | M |
| W | O | G | G | K | N | J | M | J | W | U | O | R | A | P | Y | U | I |
| Z | U | I | Q | L | E | Y | Z | N | C | R | O | A | D | G | Z | B | F |
| C | Z | F | S | W | T | I | P | G | M | G | V | N | N | N | W | J | P |
| V | S | S | M | E | V | F | U | Q | C | L | T | C | R | F | F | P | U |
| C | D | E | T | E | R | M | I | N | E | I | Y | E | J | C | Q | N | B |
| H | F | H | N | H | L | G | F | C | N | Z | U | Y | G | J | D | Y | R |
| W | G | C | V | X | V | A | L | O | R | B | R | V | L | X | T | T | N |
| C | O | M | P | L | I | A | N | T | G | P | J | M | F | E | S | E | L |

**HINT**

TOLERANCE | POWERFUL | DETERMINE | VALOR | COMPLIANT

# Word Search #6

Find the names of the 5 demons killed by Sri Rama in the following web of words.

| | | | | | | | | | | | | | | | | | |
|---|---|---|---|---|---|---|---|---|---|---|---|---|---|---|---|---|---|
| T | T | R | K | U | M | B | K | A | R | A | N | B | W | F | R | R | U |
| A | L | K | E | B | S | B | T | U | T | A | I | G | S | S | Y | S | R |
| D | R | W | A | Q | F | M | Y | M | A | R | E | E | C | H | J | K | B |
| A | Z | U | M | B | C | R | X | B | J | M | D | Z | B | Q | Y | V | R |
| K | X | P | D | D | A | C | O | N | R | Y | L | N | F | I | L | C | U |
| A | R | V | G | B | J | N | J | X | P | M | X | B | D | R | T | W | L |
| K | A | X | V | Z | G | K | D | A | S | Z | I | Q | P | I | W | C | Q |
| E | V | G | Z | S | C | F | U | H | F | Y | J | G | O | C | E | I | D |
| K | A | P | E | G | P | J | J | C | A | I | K | Y | T | B | V | Y | K |
| W | N | Z | U | E | H | X | W | H | M | E | H | I | F | V | C | J | T |
| M | A | U | W | Y | S | P | F | Q | B | F | I | L | Z | Y | F | H | B |
| A | N | K | I | X | O | L | F | W | I | F | Q | F | G | Q | S | Q | Q |

**HINT**

TADAKA | KABANDHA | MAREECH | RAVANA | KUMBKARAN

# Word Search #7

Can you spot the 5 names of Hanuman in the word maze below.

| | | | | | | | | | | | | | | | | | |
|---|---|---|---|---|---|---|---|---|---|---|---|---|---|---|---|---|---|
| W | Q | R | A | M | A | D | U | T | A | S | N | T | L | B | F | L | G |
| Y | A | Q | O | B | W | R | C | Y | G | P | I | G | B | A | G | E | P |
| O | H | X | O | Z | Y | Y | K | I | A | Y | N | M | H | Z | V | S | I |
| K | X | B | A | A | J | S | O | I | Y | M | I | I | Q | Q | N | D | A |
| A | X | S | A | D | H | T | Z | K | C | Y | L | A | A | V | Y | K | O |
| F | R | U | A | O | A | N | J | A | N | E | Y | A | M | V | C | A | B |
| M | A | H | A | V | I | R | A | T | B | H | I | L | K | T | D | J | Z |
| N | P | A | V | A | N | P | U | T | R | A | I | I | U | T | B | N | G |
| Y | C | G | R | J | S | D | T | H | W | N | Z | H | U | A | L | S | A |
| Z | E | F | B | G | G | N | T | A | I | L | Y | C | A | M | E | N | M |
| C | A | J | B | Q | X | I | C | G | G | E | Z | L | D | D | F | S | O |
| U | C | J | M | B | M | A | R | U | T | A | T | M | A | J | A | C | Q |

**HINT**

ANJANEYA | MAHAVIRA | RAMADUTA | MARUTATMAJA | PAVANPUTRA

# Word Search #8

Find the names of the 5 divine weapons used by great warriors in the Ramayana.

| | | | | | | | | | | | | | | | | | |
|---|---|---|---|---|---|---|---|---|---|---|---|---|---|---|---|---|---|
| J | A | U | D | I | C | G | I | A | M | B | F | M | Y | G | B | J | O |
| W | I | J | Z | N | A | M | G | S | A | H | N | P | F | H | F | T | M |
| J | L | E | G | D | O | W | V | Y | N | R | O | Y | Q | L | M | J | S |
| Q | R | C | H | R | Q | F | H | I | A | A | R | T | K | V | X | E | M |
| V | L | M | K | A | D | P | G | Y | V | H | A | J | L | E | Z | R | Q |
| S | M | X | F | S | W | I | R | E | A | M | Z | R | B | P | R | T | C |
| B | R | N | R | T | F | N | I | K | R | A | N | S | M | S | A | U | Q |
| X | Q | N | G | R | W | A | P | F | Y | S | L | R | B | O | P | B | L |
| W | O | I | A | A | S | K | V | M | U | T | T | Z | I | D | Q | R | V |
| P | L | T | U | E | Z | A | U | E | U | R | N | F | N | L | E | I | K |
| K | H | M | E | T | F | M | M | F | W | A | N | H | N | W | X | F | V |
| X | A | H | N | A | A | G | P | A | A | S | H | U | F | U | W | R | F |

**HINT**

PINAKA | NAAGPAASH | BHRAHMASTRA | INDRASTRA | MANAVA

# Word Search #9

From the web of words below, can you find the names of the 5 great sages from the time of the Ramayana?

| | | | | | | | | | | | | | | | | | |
|---|---|---|---|---|---|---|---|---|---|---|---|---|---|---|---|---|---|
| B | I | X | M | W | Z | T | K | W | R | J | T | F | X | X | U | S | S |
| A | R | T | I | C | B | T | H | J | X | E | L | C | S | B | T | P | N |
| U | A | J | D | M | Q | L | Y | O | R | U | I | X | C | Y | E | K | R |
| B | E | H | A | P | D | S | U | D | W | S | N | U | D | C | Y | I | I |
| Z | A | J | G | O | Y | L | M | M | B | K | U | Q | V | H | G | G | M |
| Z | P | O | A | T | R | I | Z | W | A | X | B | B | N | M | U | M | I |
| L | B | O | S | A | I | V | A | S | H | I | S | H | T | H | A | X | N |
| T | K | X | T | O | H | E | H | N | Q | J | K | W | J | G | W | U | J |
| D | S | M | Y | F | I | Q | Y | G | J | O | I | M | V | T | Q | Y | L |
| Q | Q | S | A | R | S | H | U | V | A | L | M | I | K | I | K | X | N |
| U | Y | W | P | M | Q | O | A | U | R | I | A | R | G | S | E | S | Z |
| E | A | G | A | U | T | A | M | P | V | E | Z | D | O | O | Z | B | E |

**HINT**

VALMIKI | VAISHISHTHA | GAUTAM | ATRI | AGASTYA

# Word Search #10

Ravana was a demon, but he had some great skills and qualities. Find 5 of his qualities and skills from the web of words below.

| F | S | F | X | S | L | H | G | W | O | P | W | B | I | F | S | J | F |
|---|---|---|---|---|---|---|---|---|---|---|---|---|---|---|---|---|---|
| Y | W | Z | C | C | I | P | J | Y | Q | F | D | A | H | I | P | L | H |
| Z | X | L | F | H | E | P | O | Z | P | E | U | F | R | O | V | E | S |
| D | D | M | X | O | K | S | S | L | F | G | Y | H | Y | R | M | G | H |
| E | O | U | R | L | M | W | J | S | I | N | O | W U | M | I | M | X |  |
| V | M | S | Z | A | O | E | C | N | M | T | E | X | L | O | A | O | U |
| O | Q | I | K | R | F | D | D | L | Q | Z | I | R | E | C | I | G | R |
| T | L | C | M | W | W | D | R | O | U | O | N | C | F | E | C | P | R |
| E | Y | I | Z | X | W | Y | R | X | Z | E | V | B | I | M | A | H | Z |
| E | V | A | X | Y | U | O | B | J | U | Y | G | Q | U | A | A | Z | Z |
| B | X | N | V | P | Q | G | A | M | R | G | G | T | A | U | N | C | H |
| F | R | C | H | M | Y | N | O | E | T | Q | O | T | D | M | W | L | V |

**HINT**

MUSICIAN | WARRIOR | POLITICIAN | SCHOLAR | DEVOTEE

16

# Crossword

## ARANYA KANDA

Crossword #1

Find the words based on the story of Aranya Kanda (Across and Down).

**Across**

2. Ravana's cousin, a man-eating rakshasa
4. She wanted the golden deer
8. Sita was kidnapped from _________
9. Ravana took Sita towards the _________
10. Dashanan

**Down**

1. He ran after the golden deer
2. The headless monster
3. Laxmana cut her nose
5. _________ turned into a golden deer
6. He went in search of Rama, hearing him cry in pain
7. Twin brother of Khar

# KISHKINDHA KANDA

Crossword #2

Find the words based on the story of Kishkindha Kanda (Across and Down).

**Across**

1. ________ gave the clue that Mata Sita was across the sea
4. The head of the vanara army
6. The hill where Sugriva was hiding during his exile
8. Brother of Sugriva
10. Where is Hanuman's birthplace temple in the present times
15. He asks help from Rama to get his w ife and kingdom
16. Ravana cuts his wing
17. The Asura brother of Mayavi
18. He gets angry with Sugriva for his inaction

**Down**

2. Rama and ________ became friends instantly
3. Gave Rama berries after tasting them
5. Wife of Bali
6. ________ kills Bali
7. The strongest team sent to the ________ for the search of Sita
9. Sugriva and Bali ruled
11. Son of Bali
12. Sampathi's brother
13. The vanara king
14. Wife of Sugriva

# SUNDAR KANDA

Crossword #3

## Find the words based on the story of Sundar Kanda (Across and Down).

**Across**

4. Lanka Naresh
6. Meghnad was also known as ________
9. Hanuman's mother
12. Where mata Sita was kept in Lanka
14. Ravana·s brother who joined Rama's army
15. Hanuman checked out the whole of Lanka sitting on ________ hill

**Down**

1. Mighty mountain that obstructed Hanuman on his way to Lanka
2. The rakshasi w ho guarded Sita in Lanka
3. Ravana ruled
5. Architect of Lanka
8. Hanuman's father
10. Pavan putra ________
11. The rakshasi who guarded the doors of Lanka
13. Goddess of the serpents

# YUDHA KANDA

Crossword #4

Find the words based on the story of Yudha Kanda (Across and Down).

**Across**

1. Hanuman lifts the whole mountain to get this herb
4. An army was sent to wake him up from his sleep
5. The rakshasi who dreams the defeat of Ravana
9. He was also known as Lankeshwar
12. Also known as Indrajit
13. She was waiting for Rama at Ashoka Vatika
14. Celebrated to mark the return of Rama to Ayodhya
15. Wife of Ravana
16. Son of Vishwakarma and also the engineer of the Rama Setu

**Down**

1. He tells Rama not to t rust Vibhishana
2. He was crowned the king after Ravana's death
3. The Rama Setu was built from Rameshwaram to reach _________
6. Ravana's maternal grandfather
7. The place where Rama built the Rama Setu
8. Celebrated for the demise of Ravana
10. The name of the bridge built from Rameshwaram to Lanka
11. He challenged all Ravana 's courtiers to just move his leg

# DASHRATHA

Crossword #5

Find the words based on the life of King Dashratha (Across and Down).

**Across**

5. Dashratha's queen, the good friend
9. How many members of Dashratha's family were exiled?
10. Dashratha mistook ________ to be an animal thus accidentally killed him
11. Ten chariots
13. Raghukul reet sada chali aayi praan jaye par ________ na jaye
14. Dashratha's kul-guru
16. Dashratha's daughters-in-law came from the kingdom of ________
17. Dashratha's wife who saved him in a battle

**Down**

1. Which yagna did Dashratha perform to beget a son
2. Dashratha's father-in-law, the lord of the horses
3. Capital of Dashratha's kingdom was the city of ________
4. Dashratha's minister who went to drop Sita, Rama and Lakshmana to the outskirts of the city when they were exiled
6. ________ was the hunchback in Dashratha's kingdom
7. Which sage performed the yagna for Dashratha?
8. How many sons did Dashratha have?
12. Dashratha ruled the kingdom of ________
15. Dashrath could shoot any target just by hearing the ________

# RAMA

Find the words based on the life of Lord Rama (Across and Down).

Crossword #6

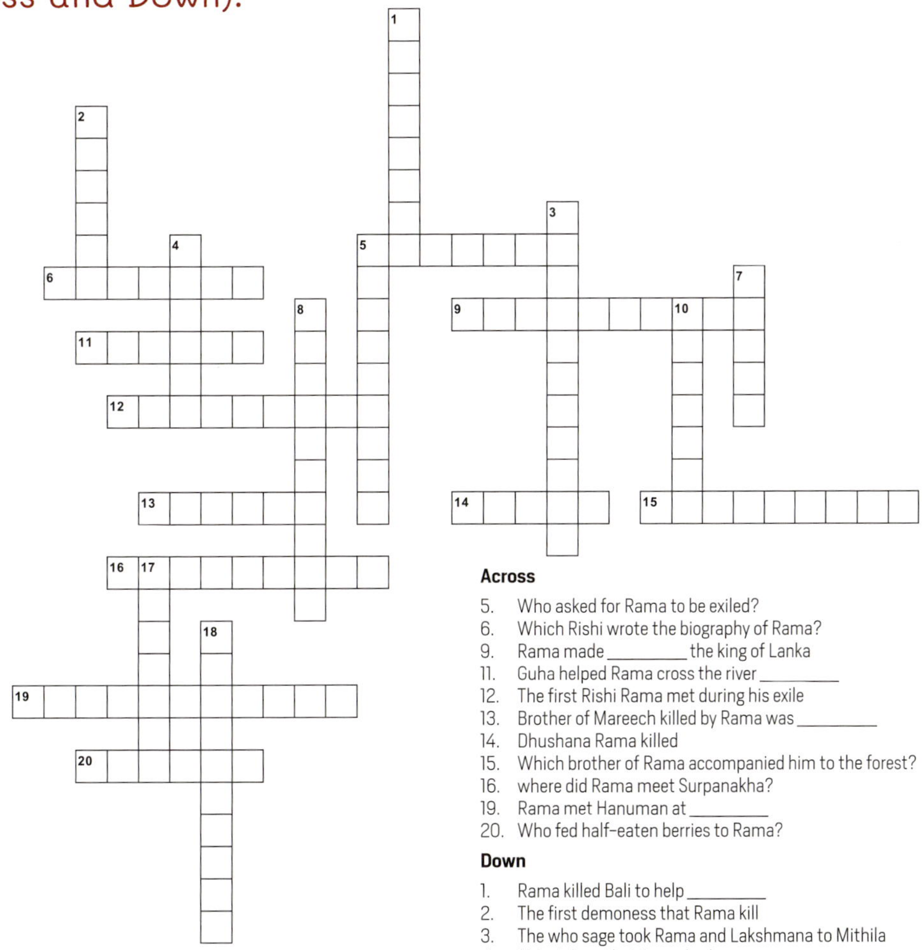

**Across**

5. Who asked for Rama to be exiled?
6. Which Rishi wrote the biography of Rama?
9. Rama made _________ the king of Lanka
11. Guha helped Rama cross the river _________
12. The first Rishi Rama met during his exile
13. Brother of Mareech killed by Rama was _________
14. Dhushana Rama killed
15. Which brother of Rama accompanied him to the forest?
16. where did Rama meet Surpanakha?
19. Rama met Hanuman at _________
20. Who fed half-eaten berries to Rama?

**Down**

1. Rama killed Bali to help _________
2. The first demoness that Rama kill
3. The who sage took Rama and Lakshmana to Mithila
4. Shiva's bow that Rama broke
5. Who was Rama's mother?
7. In which city did the Rama-Ravana war happen?
8. Who was angry when Rama broke shiva's bow?
10. The rishi who gave weapons to Rama before his battle with Ravana
17. Where was Rama born?
18. Where did Rama and Bharata meet when Rama was in exile?

# SITA

Crossword #7

Find the words based on the life of Mata Sita (Across and Down).

**Across**

5. Sita was princess of the kingdom of ________
7. Who is is also called Bhoomija?
8. Who is also known as Siyavar?
9. Sita's father
10. Sita became the queen of ________ Kingdom
12. Who tricked Sita in the guise of a golden deer?
13. Where was Sita born ?
14. While Sita was in Lanka she lived in ________

**Down**

1. What ornament of hers did Sita give Hanuman when she met him in Lanka?
2. Ravana took Sita to Lanka in ________
3. Sita's friend and confidant in Lanka
5. Kanak Bhavan was gifted to Rama and Sita by ________
6. Sita being the princess of Videha was also knows as ________
11. Ravana disguised himself as a ________ to abduct Sita

# HANUMAN

Crossword #8

## Find the words based on the life of Lord Hanuman (Across and Down).

**Across**

2. Hanuman first met Rama and Lakshmana disguised as a ________
3. The naga maiden who obstructed Hanuman on his way to Lanka
5. Bird who informed Hanuman about Sita being in Lanka
9. Ravana's son killed by Hanuman when he visited Lanka in search of Sita
10. Hanuman's birthplace
11. Hanuman was the son of ________ god
13. Who stops Hanuman from entering Lanka at its gates?
14. Jai Hanuman Gyan Gun Sagar Jai ________ Teehu Lok Ujagar
15. Vanara King ________ was introduced by Hanuman to Rama

**Down**

1. Indrajeet used ________ weapon to bind Hanuman
4. ________ inspired Hanuman to cross the ocean to Lanka
6. Hanuman's father
7. Who is also known as Anajaneya ?
8. Hanuman misunderstood ________ to be a fruit in his childhood and thus ate it
12. ________ advises Ravana against killing Hanuman

# 17 Emoji Quiz

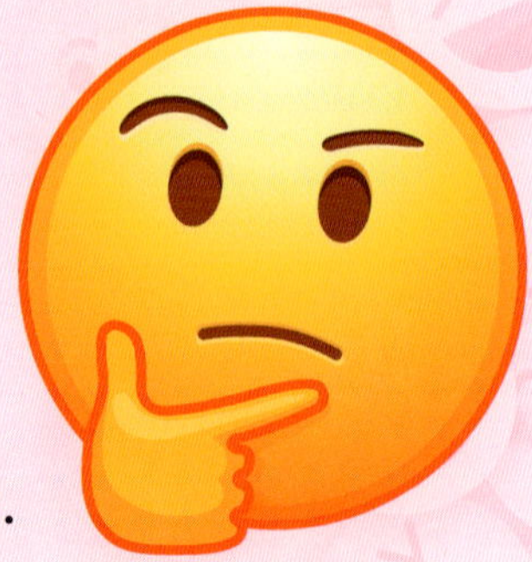

Identify these Ramayana characters and places.

1.  ..........................................

2.  ..........................................

3.  ..........................................

4.  ..........................................

5.  ..........................................

6.  ..........................................

7.  ..........................................

8. 

9. 

10.  Y A

11. 

12. 

13. 

14. 

15. 

16. 

17.  N

18. ☁ ✖ D ..............................

19. 👁 🎨 ✌ ..............................

20. ★ ..............................

21. 💕 ..............................

22. ⚫ 🤝 ..............................

23.  ➕ ℹ ..............................

24. ✋ ➕ 🌳 ..............................

25.  👂 D A ..............................

26. K A ..............................

27. 🌹 K ✈ ..............................

28.  ____________________

29.  ____________________

30.  ____________________

18

# Colour the Madhubani Art

Madhubani Art is said to date back to the time of Ramayana, when King Janaka asked an artist to capture his daughter Sita's wedding to Prince Rama. These paintings were usually created on walls and floors of homes during festivals, ceremonies, or special occasions. Having originated in the Mithila region of Bihar, this form of painting is also known as Mithila Painting.

# RAMA AND SITA'S MARRIAGE

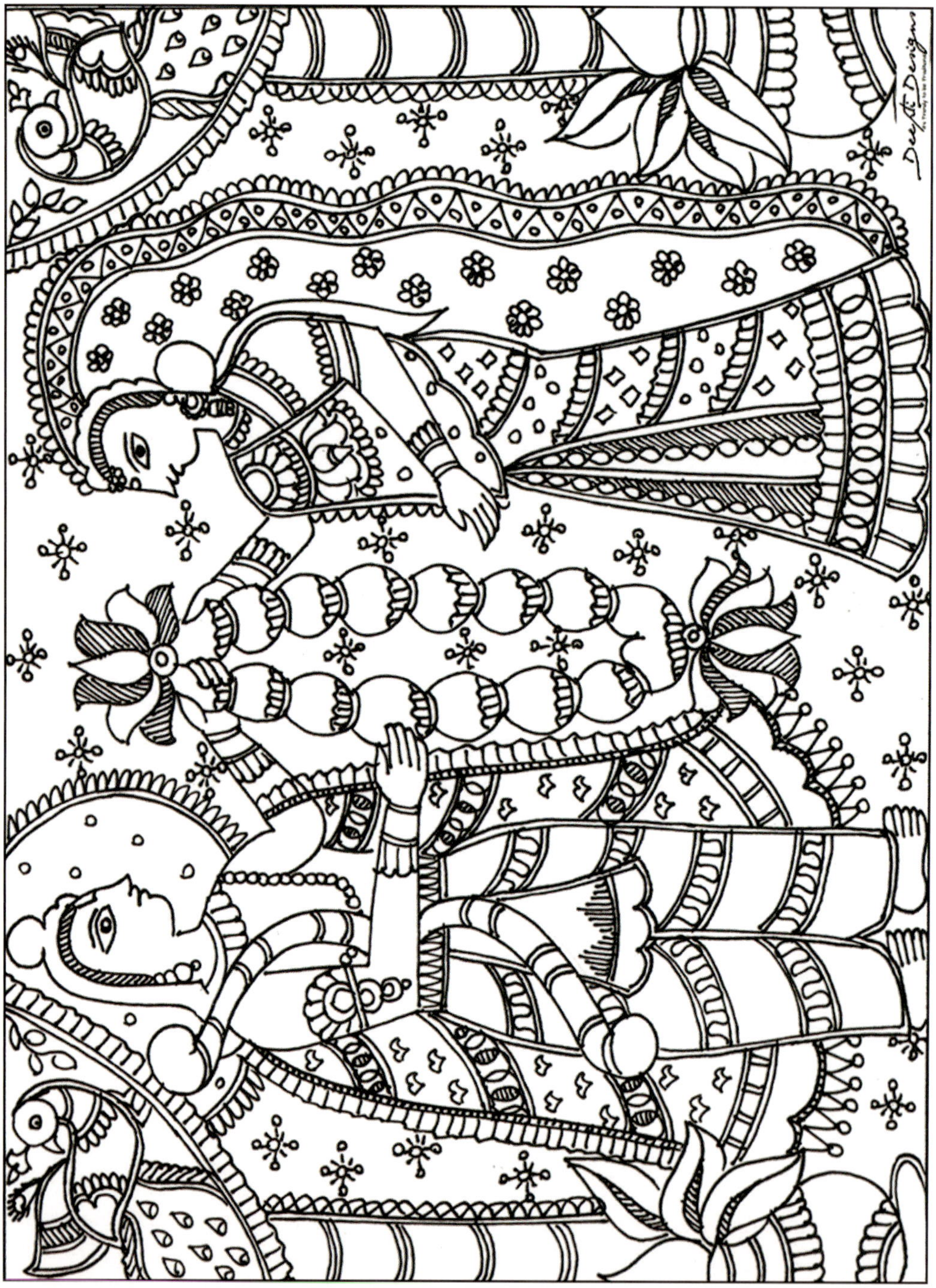

# RAMA, SITA, AND LAXMANA GOING FOR VANVASA (EXILE)

# LAXMANA CUTTING OFF SURPANAKHA'S NOSE AND EARS

# BALI AND SUGRIVA'S FIGHT

## HANUMAN FINDS MATA SITA

## RAMA KILLS RAVANA

# C Think and Reflect

## Reflection 1

By now, you are quite an expert on Ramayana. Write the story of Ramayana in your own words in the space below.

## Reflection 2

Who is your favourite character in Ramayana and why?

## Reflection 3

Within each of us, there are qualities of both Rama and Ravana. Let us identify and nurture our Rama qualities, while working to eliminate our Ravana qualities. The first step on this journey is self-awareness, that is, understanding and identifying these qualities within us. Why don't you list them both here.

| My Rama qualities | My Ravana qualities |
|---|---|
| 1. ________ | 1. ________ |
| 2. ________ | 2. ________ |
| 3. ________ | 3. ________ |
| 4. ________ | 4. ________ |
| 5. ________ | 5. ________ |
| 6. ________ | 6. ________ |
| 7. ________ | 7. ________ |
| 8. ________ | 8. ________ |
| 9. ________ | 9. ________ |
| 10. ________ | 10. ________ |

D

# Answer Key

# BALA KANDA

**1. Fill in the blanks:**

(a) Kausalya (b) Kaikeyi (c) Sumitra (d) Putra-Kameshti (e) Rama (f) Lakshmana (g) Satrughna (h) Bharata (i) Vishwamitra (j) Maricha (k) Subahu (l) Tadaka (m) Maricha (n) Subahu (o) Janaka (p) Shiva (q) Rama

**2. Quiz challenge:**

1. a) Rishi Valmiki
2. c) 645
3. a) 24,000
4. b) Lord Vishnu
5. b) Seven
6. c) Sarayu
7. c) Sarayu
8. d) Solar Dynasty
9. a) King Manu
10. a) Sage Vashistha
11. d) Itihasa
12. b) Sumitra
13. c) Punarvasu
14. b) Kaushalya
15. d) PutraKameshti Yagna
16. b) Rishi Rishyasringa
17. d) Sage Vishwamitra
18. a) Sagar
19. b) A vessel of payasam (milk pudding)
20. b) Kingdom of Kosala"
21. a) Ayodhya
22. d) Uttar Pradesh
23. c) Tadaka
24. d) Rishi Bhardwaj
25. c) King Janaka
26. c) Rama Navami
27. c) Ayodhya
28. c) Bhagwan Vishnu
29. b) Urmila
30. c) Mareech
31. c) Bhagwan Parashuram
32. c) Eka Patni Vrata (One Life, One Wife)
33. c) Sruthakeerthi
34. a) Mandavi
35. b) Kaikeyi
36. a) Sarayu
37. b) Tadka
38. c) Aranya Kand
39. c) Rama
40. a) Ayodhya Kand

# AYODHYA KANDA

**3. Fill in the blanks:**

a) Rama, b) King Dashratha, c) Coronation, d) Manthara, e) Kaikeyi, f) Boons g) Bharata, h) Rama i) 14 years of Exile to Rama, j) Sita, k) Lakshman, l) Guha, m) Saryu, n) Kaikeyi, o) Rama p) Guha q) Bhardwaja, r) Chitrakoot, s) Kingship t) Nandigrama

**4. Quiz challenge:**

1. b) Rama's qualities to lead and care were appreciated by everyone
2. b) Her father was the king of Kekeya Kingdom
3. c) Ashwapati
4. d) Manthara
5. b) Vanvasa for Rama and kingship for Bharata
6. b) Dasaratha
7. b) Laxman and Sita
8. a) Sumantra
9. b) Guha
10. b) Rishi Bhardawaj
11. b) Tamasa
12. c) Chitrakoot
13. d) Shravana Kumar
14. b) ...that Bharat is coming to kill Rama, so that he can never return
15. c) Rishi Vashishtha
16. a) With Rama's padukas (sandals) on the throne, Bharata lived in a hut in a village
17. d) Asked his charioteer to create multiple misleading tyre marks of the chariot
18. c) Rishi Bhardawaj
19. c) They expressed sorrow and tried to follow him.
20. b) When Dashratha killed Shravana Kumar
21. c) Sent messengers to call for Bharat and Shatrugan
22. a) Away at their maternal grand father's home at Kekeya
23. c) Large number of citizens, army, gurus, ministers, and all the family members
24. b) He fainted in sorrow and grief
25. d) Rishi Jabali
26. b) Tapasavi
27. a) Rishi Atri
28. a) Anasuya
29. b) How to play the role of a devoted wife
30. c) Aranya Kanda
31. c) He gave them a speech about his duty and honour
32. a) Bharat Milap Temple
33. c) Kaikeyi
34. d) Rama's Charan Paduka (footwear)
35. c) Fear of losing power and status
36. a) Shesha Naga, the snake that sheltered Bhagwan Vishnu
37. b) Shatrughna
38. a) Uttar Pradesh
39. c) He respectfully accepted his father's order
40. d) Aranya Kanda

# ARANYA KANAD

**5. Fill in the blanks:**

a) Augustya b) Panchvati, c) Surpanakha, d) Marry e) Nose and ears, f) Khara and Dushan, g) Ravana h) Mareecha, i) Rekha j) Jatayu, k) South

**6. Quiz challenge:**

1. a) 12
2. c) Dandaka forest
3. b) Rishi Agastya
4. a) It has 5 Banyan trees (Panch Vat Vriksha)
5. c) Godavari
6. a) Maharashtra
7. c) Surpanakha
8. b) Khara-Dushan
9. c) Mareech
10. a) Panchvati
11. d) Golden deer
12. c) Jatayu
13. c) Ravana abducted her and took her towards south
14. c) Arrows
15. b) Vishrava Muni
16. b) Message in favour of monogamy
17. d ) 14,000 demons
18. b) Mareech warned Ravana against adducting Sita
19. d) Jatayu
20. d) Mareech
21. d) Surpanakha
22. d) Kabandha
23. b) Laxmana
24. b) Sugreeva
25. c) Godavari
26. Aruna (the charioteer of the sun god Surya)
27. b) Laxmana
28. a) Mareech, golden deer, Panchvati
29. c) Ravana decided to abduct Sita
30. b) Shabari
31. b) She wanted to check the sweetness of the fruits before offering
32. a) Kabandha
33. c) Pampa Lake
34. a) 3 eyes
35. c) Rama
36. b) He accepts her hospitality
37. d) Rama
38. a) Stomach
39. c) She sat on the funeral fire
40. b) Kishkinda Kanda

# KISHKINDA KANDA

**7. Fill in the blanks:**

b) Sita, c) Kishkinda c) Rishimukh d) Hanuman e) Bali, f) Brahmin g) Language h) Garland i) Ruma j) Angad k) Vanar (l) Jambavan m) Sampati (n) Ashoka Vatika

**8. Quiz challenge:**

1. b) 67
2. c) Sampati
3. c) Brothers
4. d) Karnataka
5. a) Saint
6. a) Indra Deva
7. b) Tara
8. c) Rishimukha Hill
9. c) Fire
10. b) Mayavi
11. a) Tara
12. a) Ruma
13. b) Angada
14. a) Rishi Matanga
15. c) Jambavan
16. c) Finger ring
17. b) Both were away from their kingdom and their wives
18. c) Mainaka hills
19. a) Brothers
20. b) Vali
21. b) The abduction of Sita
22. d) Rishimukha hills
23. a) Tara
24. c) Acharya Tulsidas
25. a) Kesari
26. b) Anjana
27. c) Vayu Deva
28. c) Karnataka
29. c) His intellect and great communication skills
30. a) Sugriiva aaj-na 'the inviolable order of Sugreeva'
31. b) South
32. b) South
33. d) Somagiri Mountain
34. c) Astagiri Mountain
35. a) Udaya Mountain
36. b) Mahendra Mountains
37. d) Sanskrit
38. b) To help find Sita
39. b) As a symbol to establish Mata Sita's trust
40. c) Arjun

# SUNDAR KANDA

**9. Fill in the blanks:**

a) Jambavan, b) Mainaka c) Surasa d) Vishwakarma e) Lankini (f) Sita (g) Ravana (h) Rama's story (i) Ring (j) Chudamani (hair clip) (k) Ashoka Vatika (l) Akshay Kumar (m) Indrajeet (n) Brahmastra (o) Vibhishana (p) Tail (q) One-third

**10. Quiz challenge:**

1. a) Mace
2. c) Sun
3. a) Sage
4. a) His mother, Anjana
5. c) Hampi, Karnataka
6. d) Jambavan
7. b) Ashok Vatika
8. d) Crest jewel
9. a) Mata Sita
10. b) 40 Chaupais
11. b) Mainaka
12. a) Sursa
13. a) Lankini
14. c) Vibhishan
15. d) All of the above
16. b) By singing the story of Rama
17. c) Trikuta Mountain
18. b) "Bhoot pishach nikat nahi aave"
19. c) Akshay Kumar
20. c) Assessing strengths, weaknesses and fortification of Lanka
21. a) Indrajeet's Brahmastra
22. d) Nikumbha
23. c) An ardent devotee of Rama
24. c) Bheem
25. c) Aurangzeb
26. a) "Rama doot"
27. c) Vishwakarma
28. a) That Rama will come soon to save her
29. b) Started creating havoc at Ashoka Vatika
30. d) Indrajeet
31. b) By setting fire to his tail
32. d) Vibhishan
33. a) Beautiful and prosperous
34. c) 3 (2 in starting and 1 in the end)
35. c) Sheshnag
36. c) Anima
37. c) Ravana asked his soldiers to kill Hanuman
38. b) Hanuman
39. c) With Hanuman's return to Rama
40. d) Trijata

# YUDHA KANDA

**11. Fill in the blanks:**

(a) Hanuman (b) Vibhishana (c) Maricha (d) Mandodari (e) Kumbhkaran (f) Malyavan (g) Lanka (h) Rama (i) Sugriva (j) Hanuman (k) Sea (l) Arrows (m) Nala (n) Neel (o) Rama Setu (p) Four (q) Angada (r) Indrajit (s) Kumbhkaran (t) Rama (u) Varana (v) Sanjeevani (w) Brahmastra (x) Vibhishana (y) Dussehra (z) Diwali

**12. Quiz challenge:**

1. c) Nala
2. a) 30 miles
3. b) Musician
4. a) Treta Yuga
5. c) Vibhishan
6. d) 10
7. a) Prahasta
8. b) Kuber
9. c) Dhanyamalini
10. d) Seven (Meghanada, Atikaya, Akshayakumara, Narantaka, Devantaka, Trishira, and Prahasta)
11. b) Dronagiri
12. d) Shuka and Sarana
13. a) Trijata
14. b) Maternal grandfather
15. c) Laxmana
16. d) Hanuman
17. a) Indrajeet
18. c) Hanuman
19. b) Nagpash
20. d) Bhagwan Brahma
21. a) Rama
22. c) Hanuman
23. a) Sanjeevani
24. a) Laxmana
25. c) Pushpaka Vimana
26. b) Mandoduri
27. a) Trident
28. d) Arrow
29. b) Akshaya Kumar
30. a) Laxmana
31. c) Neel
32. a) Rama
33. d) Tadaka
34. c) Bali
35. b) Kumbhakaran
36. b) Sushen
37. d) Rishi Visharva and Mata Kaikesi
38. b) Indra
39. a) Vibhishana
40. c) Vibhishana

# 13. SEQUENCE THE STORY

1. b) c, d, b, a
2. d) c, b, d, a
3. d) d, a, c, b
4. b) a, c, d, b
5. c) d, c, a, b
6. a) a, b, d, c
7. a) a, b, d, c
8. c) d, b, a, c
9. b) a, b, c, d
10. a) d, a, b, c
11. d) a, b, d, c
12. c) b, a, d, c
13. a) c, a, d, b
14. b) a, c, b, d
15. c) a, d, b, c
16. b) a, c, b, d
17. d) b, c, a, d
18. a) b, a, d, c
19. a) b, a, d, c
20. d) d, c, a, b

# 14. MAZE SOLUTIONS

Maze #1

Maze #2

Maze #3

Maze #4

Maze #5

Bharata should follow path 'C' to reach his brother Rama.

Maze #6

Maze #7

Maze #8

## Maze #9

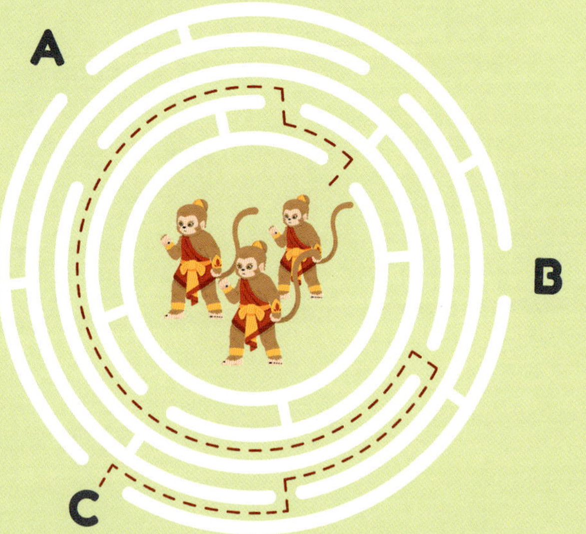


## Maze #10

Maze #11

# 15. WORD SEARCH

Word Search #1

| | | | | | | | | | | | | | | | | | |
|---|---|---|---|---|---|---|---|---|---|---|---|---|---|---|---|---|---|
| X | Z | Q | T | G | U | U | R | O | E | Z | T | R | S | Q | R | A | O |
| I | L | M | O | L | H | A | P | E | J | J | Z | T | X | G | N | W | T |
| U | J | C | F | K | R | X | T | Q | S | D | L | R | Z | Q | X | N | X |
| A | Q | H | F | F | H | K | B | U | W | P | B | G | R | F | I | C | Y |
| W | P | Q | C | V | Q | Z | A | O | W | H | O | E | S | N | P | Q | D |
| H | Z | A | I | K | R | N | J | T | Q | L | Z | N | Y | O | H | D | L |
| O | L | O | R | J | V | F | I | U | K | D | U | F | S | T | R | V | X |
| N | B | O | B | E | D | I | E | N | T | V | E | G | K | I | Y | K | R |
| E | A | S | O | Y | T | Z | V | N | R | Z | T | Z | I | N | B | K | R |
| S | U | S | E | H | I | Z | H | L | Q | Q | I | U | N | Q | X | L | I |
| T | X | K | B | N | U | G | A | I | A | B | N | T | D | Q | W | R | E |
| R | O | T | R | U | T | H | F | U | L | G | C | S | H | G | E | S | E |

Word Search #2

| | | | | | | | | | | | | | | | | | |
|---|---|---|---|---|---|---|---|---|---|---|---|---|---|---|---|---|---|
| Q | F | S | H | A | B | A | R | I | T | A | N | P | D | G | U | G | V |
| F | D | D | B | J | G | I | B | Y | X | A | Z | U | H | Q | F | X | V |
| A | F | R | J | X | H | C | H | D | Z | U | B | K | P | Q | Z | K | Q |
| F | G | R | A | Z | T | L | S | U | G | R | E | E | V | A | K | A | I |
| Z | Q | H | I | M | J | H | S | C | R | E | T | L | L | V | E | F | J |
| M | K | A | T | M | A | K | I | S | H | K | I | N | D | A | I | T | S |
| Q | H | N | V | W | M | F | D | F | I | Y | J | L | Y | U | B | O | U |
| L | O | U | V | I | B | H | E | E | S | H | A | N | A | Y | T | U | T |
| M | L | M | C | H | D | C | R | A | Y | O | D | H | Y | A | Q | D | L |
| G | V | A | L | A | K | S | H | M | A | N | A | J | L | H | H | B | T |
| U | L | N | S | H | K | C | F | U | D | N | V | B | W | W | F | U | I |
| R | X | X | A | K | E | V | A | T | H | Q | K | F | D | R | W | R | P |

## Word Search #3

| A | A | E | P | Z | L | D | B | J | Q | H | H | S | D | V | S | T | T |
|---|---|---|---|---|---|---|---|---|---|---|---|---|---|---|---|---|---|
| J | A | N | K | I | Y | N | H | C | D | J | D | I | C | F | U | K | D |
| S | R | E | F | U | J | I | O | N | Y | V | B | X | N | L | I | V | A |
| I | V | J | E | K | S | T | O | R | C | Y | O | G | L | X | K | K | X |
| H | A | Y | B | U | E | F | M | W | W | P | E | B | Z | X | F | X | W |
| C | I | P | X | H | E | Q | I | W | R | O | U | O | F | G | B | B | Y |
| T | D | N | O | T | U | V | K | L | I | I | V | P | G | N | N | V | V |
| N | H | F | T | Y | N | M | M | A | I | T | H | I | L | I | A | O | G |
| N | E | Z | Z | Q | S | N | I | K | P | G | T | Y | O | U | D | N | X |
| G | Z | B | J | X | W | P | R | J | Y | A | S | P | R | Y | E | D | K |
| S | I | D | X | A | V | O | Y | A | A | E | Z | H | I | Z | M | K | C |
| D | D | X | T | J | L | R | L | Y | Y | X | L | M | D | G | O | L | W |

## Word Search #4

| Z | R | R | R | K | R | E | B | K | L | F | I | Z | Q | S | U | V | B |
|---|---|---|---|---|---|---|---|---|---|---|---|---|---|---|---|---|---|
| H | T | W | U | L | G | E | K | O | S | W | I | S | E | P | H | W | R |
| J | A | N | R | R | K | H | B | O | S | O | E | V | L | Q | J | L | A |
| E | A | J | G | H | R | G | H | I | T | Z | C | B | B | D | O | H | V |
| S | T | O | V | M | D | G | D | S | R | H | F | E | W | W | U | U | E |
| G | W | J | L | X | I | J | X | L | E | P | F | H | D | N | Y | M | Q |
| X | M | V | R | D | R | L | Y | I | N | S | F | R | Q | F | G | I | S |
| K | N | X | J | S | T | Q | P | L | G | D | E | D | C | N | E | L | E |
| S | C | B | U | K | Q | R |  | O | T | H | C | Q | W | D | W | I | U |
| W | R | S | E | M | A | U | W | R | H | R | U | P | B | O | X | T | N |
| D | Q | S | F | W | V | F | L | O | Y | A | L | T | Y | F | W | Y | V |
| G | R | P | F | P | V | X | L | W | G | C | Z | V | B | A | A | C | C |

## Word Search #5

| G | R | O | A | F | G | X | V | V | G | W | B | T | W | W | E | B | L |
|---|---|---|---|---|---|---|---|---|---|---|---|---|---|---|---|---|---|
| R | O | I | X | P | O | W | E | R | F | U | L | O | P | N | B | Q | D |
| R | D | D | K | Q | B | P | X | F | X | P | V | L | M | K | R | G | W |
| Z | X | Y | F | O | I | J | K | E | C | V | A | E | B | E | E | F | M |
| W | O | G | G | K | N | J | M | J | W | U | O | R | A | P | Y | U | I |
| Z | U | I | Q | L | E | Y | Z | N | C | R | O | A | D | G | Z | B | F |
| C | Z | F | S | W | T | I | P | G | M | G | V | N | N | N | W | J | P |
| V | S | S | M | E | V | F | U | Q | C | L | T | C | R | F | F | P | U |
| C | D | E | T | E | R | M | I | N | E | I | Y | E | J | C | Q | N | B |
| H | F | H | N | H | L | G | F | C | N | Z | U | Y | G | J | D | Y | R |
| W | G | C | V | X | V | A | L | O | R | B | R | V | L | X | T | T | N |
| C | O | M | P | L | I | A | N | T | G | P | J | M | F | E | S | E | L |

## Word Search #6

| T | T | R | K | U | M | B | K | A | R | A | N | B | W | F | R | R | U |
|---|---|---|---|---|---|---|---|---|---|---|---|---|---|---|---|---|---|
| A | L | K | E | B | S | B | T | U | T | A | I | G | S | S | Y | S | R |
| D | R | W | A | Q | F | M | Y | M | A | R | E | E | C | H | J | K | B |
| A | Z | U | M | B | C | R | X | B | J | M | D | Z | B | Q | Y | V | R |
| K | X | P | D | D | A | C | O | N | R | Y | L | N | F | I | L | C | U |
| A | R | V | G | B | J | N | J | X | P | M | X | B | D | R | T | W | L |
| K | A | X | V | Z | G | K | D | A | S | Z | I | Q | P | I | W | C | Q |
| E | V | G | Z | S | C | F | U | H | F | Y | J | G | O | C | E | I | D |
| K | A | P | E | G | P | J | J | C | A | I | K | Y | T | B | V | Y | K |
| W | N | Z | U | E | H | X | W | H | M | E | H | I | F | V | C | J | T |
| M | A | U | W | Y | S | P | F | Q | B | F | I | L | Z | Y | F | H | B |
| A | N | K | I | X | O | L | F | W | I | F | Q | F | G | Q | S | Q | Q |

## Word Search #7

| W | Q | R | A | M | A | D | U | T | A | S | N | T | L | B | F | L | G |
|---|---|---|---|---|---|---|---|---|---|---|---|---|---|---|---|---|---|
| Y | A | Q | O | B | W | R | C | Y | G | P | I | G | B | A | G | E | P |
| O | H | X | O | Z | Y | Y | K | I | A | Y | N | M | H | Z | V | S | I |
| K | X | B | A | A | J | S | O | I | Y | M | I | I | Q | Q | N | D | A |
| A | X | S | A | D | H | T | Z | K | C | Y | L | A | A | V | Y | K | O |
| F | R | U | A | O | A | N | J | A | N | E | Y | A | M | V | C | A | B |
| M | A | H | A | V | I | R | A | T | B | H | I | L | K | T | D | J | Z |
| N | P | A | V | A | N | P | U | T | R | A | I | I | U | T | B | N | G |
| Y | C | G | R | J | S | D | T | H | W | N | Z | H | U | A | L | S | A |
| Z | E | F | B | G | G | N | T | A | I | L | Y | C | A | M | E | N | M |
| C | A | J | B | Q | X | I | C | G | G | E | Z | L | D | D | F | S | O |
| U | C | J | M | B | M | A | R | U | T | A | T | M | A | J | A | C | Q |

## Word Search #8

| J | A | U | D | I | C | G | I | A | M | B | F | M | Y | G | B | J | O |
|---|---|---|---|---|---|---|---|---|---|---|---|---|---|---|---|---|---|
| W | I | J | Z | N | A | M | G | S | A | H | N | P | F | H | F | T | M |
| J | L | E | G | D | O | W | V | Y | N | R | O | Y | Q | L | M | J | S |
| Q | R | C | H | R | Q | F | H | I | A | A | R | T | K | V | X | E | M |
| V | L | M | K | A | D | P | G | Y | V | H | A | J | L | E | Z | R | Q |
| S | M | X | F | S | W | I | R | E | A | M | Z | R | B | P | R | T | C |
| B | R | N | R | T | F | N | I | K | R | A | N | S | M | S | A | U | Q |
| X | Q | N | G | R | W | A | P | F | Y | S | L | R | B | O | P | B | L |
| W | O | I | A | A | S | K | V | M | U | T | T | Z | I | D | Q | R | V |
| P | L | T | U | E | Z | A | U | E | U | R | N | F | N | L | E | I | K |
| K | H | M | E | T | F | M | M | F | W | A | N | H | N | W | X | F | V |
| X | A | H | N | A | A | G | P | A | A | S | H | U | F | U | W | R | F |

## Word Search #9

| B | I | X | M | W | Z | T | K | W | R | J | T | F | X | X | U | S | S |
|---|---|---|---|---|---|---|---|---|---|---|---|---|---|---|---|---|---|
| A | R | T | I | C | B | T | H | J | X | E | L | C | S | B | T | P | N |
| U | A | J | D | M | Q | L | Y | O | R | U | I | X | C | Y | E | K | R |
| B | E | H | A | P | D | S | U | D | W | S | N | U | D | C | Y | I | I |
| Z | A | J | G | O | Y | L | M | M | B | K | U | Q | V | H | G | G | M |
| Z | P | O | A | T | R | I | Z | W | A | X | B | B | N | M | U | M | I |
| L | B | O | S | A | I | V | A | S | H | I | S | H | T | H | A | X | N |
| T | K | X | T | O | H | E | H | N | Q | J | K | W | J | G | W | U | J |
| D | S | M | Y | F | I | Q | Y | G | J | O | I | M | V | T | Q | Y | L |
| Q | Q | S | A | R | S | H | U | V | A | L | M | I | K | I | K | X | N |
| U | Y | W | P | M | Q | O | A | U | R | I | A | R | G | S | E | S | Z |
| E | A | G | A | U | T | A | M | P | V | E | Z | D | O | O | Z | B | E |

## Word Search #10

| F | S | F | X | S | L | H | G | W | O | P | W | B | I | F | S | J | F |
|---|---|---|---|---|---|---|---|---|---|---|---|---|---|---|---|---|---|
| Y | W | Z | C | C | I | P | J | Y | Q | F | D | A | H | I | P | L | H |
| Z | X | L | F | H | E | P | O | Z | P | E | U | F | R | O | V | E | S |
| D | D | M | X | O | K | S | S | L | F | G | Y | H | Y | R | M | G | H |
| E | O | U | R | L | M | W | J | S | I | N | O | W | M | I | I | X | U |
| V | M | S | Z | A | O | E | C | N | M | T | E | X | L | O | A | O | U |
| O | Q | I | K | R | F | D | D | L | Q | Z | I | R | E | C | I | G | R |
| T | L | C | M | W | W | D | R | O | U | O | N | C | F | E | C | P | R |
| E | Y | I | Z | X | W | Y | R | X | Z | E | V | B | I | M | A | H | Z |
| E | V | A | X | Y | U | O | B | J | U | Y | G | Q | U | A | A | Z | Z |
| B | X | N | V | P | Q | G | A | M | R | G | G | T | A | U | N | C | H |
| F | R | C | H | M | Y | N | O | E | T | Q | O | T | D | M | W | L | V |

# 16. CROSSWORD SOLUTIONS

Crossword #1

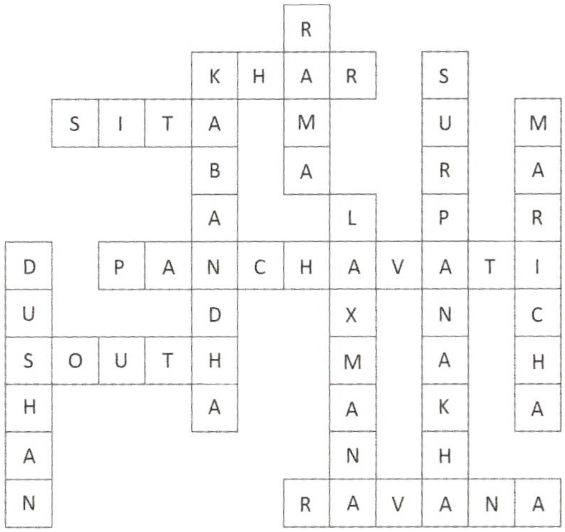


Crossword #2

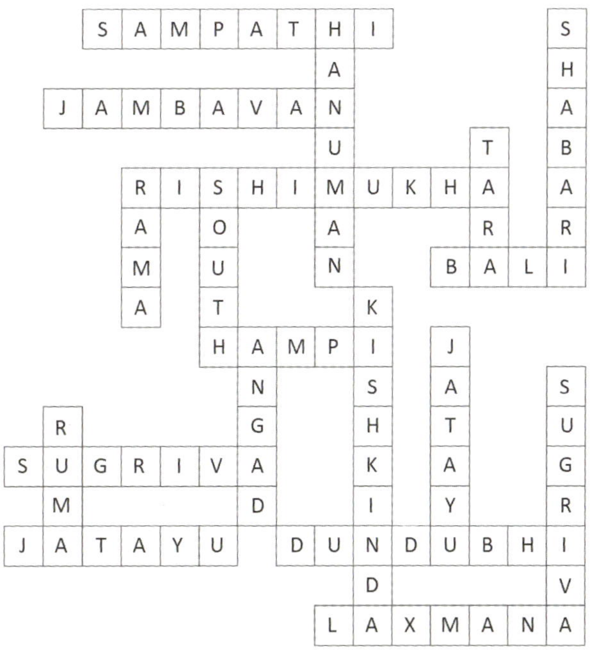

## Crossword #3

## Crossword #4

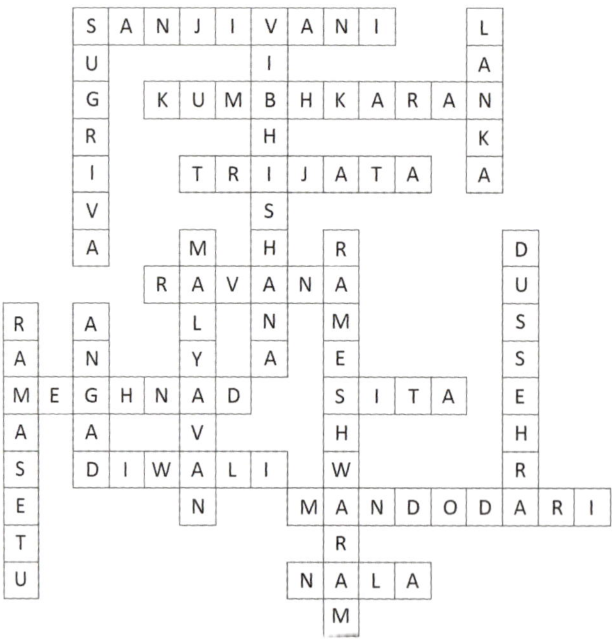

## Crossword #5

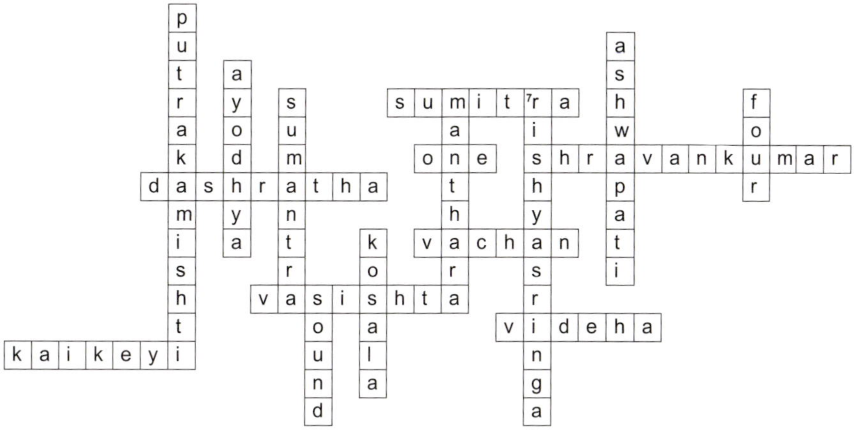


## Crossword #6

## Crossword #7

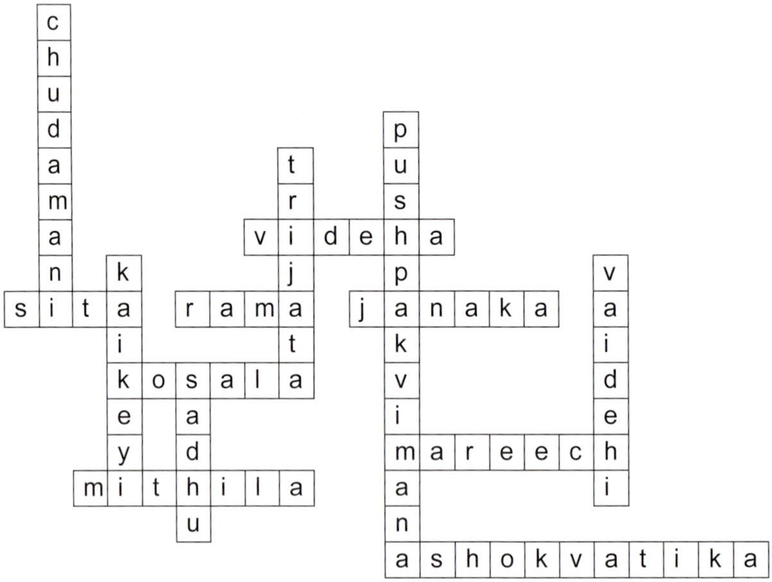


## Crossword #8

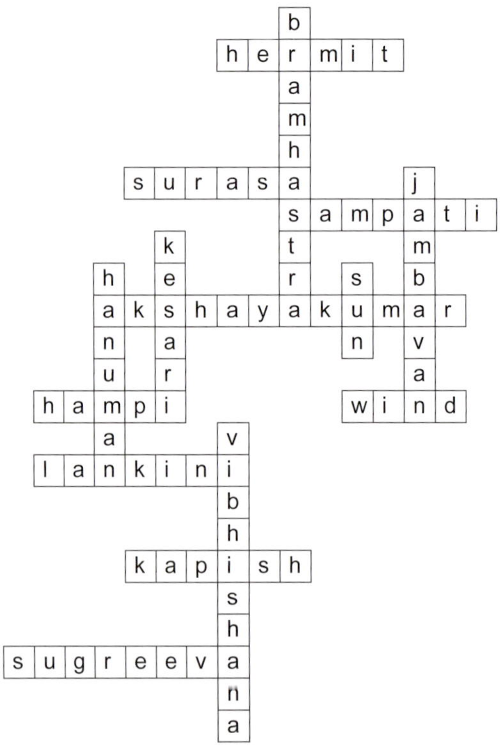

# 17. EMOJI QUIZ SOLUTIONS

1. R + Aam = Rama
2. Lakshya + Man = Laxmana
3. Bharat
4. Shatru + GUN = Shatrughan
5. Sea + Tata = Sita
6. Haan + Naa + Man = Hanuman
7. Maruti Logo = Maruti (Another Name of Hanuman)
8. Das + Rath = Dashrath
9. R + Van = Ravan
10. Cow + Shell + Ya = Kaushalya
11. Sui + Mitra = Sumitra
12. Cake + Eye - Kaikeyi
13. Man + Thoda = Manthara
14. V (Victory) + Bee + Sun = Vibhishan
15. Ja + Ta (Tata) + You = Jatayu
16. Jamun + Van = Jambavan
17. Kumbh + Car + N = Kumbhkaran
18. Megh + Na + D = Meghanad
19. I (Eye) + Draw + Jeet = Indrajeet
20. Star = Tara (Wife of Bali)
21. Love = Luv (Son of Rama & Sita)
22. Vishwa + Mitra = Vishwamitra
23. Bal (Hair) + I = Bali
24. Panch + Vat (Banyan Tree) = Panchvati
25. Kesh + Kan + Da = Kishkinda
26. Tata + Ka = Tataka
27. Pushp + K + Viman = Pushpak Viman
28. Bal + Mic + I = Valmiki
29. Sur + Paan + Kha = Surpanakha
30. Man + Do (Number 2) + Door + I
    = Mandodari

# IDENTIFY THE NAMES IN THE PICTURE SOLUTIONS

### 1. NAME ALL THE THE AVTARS OF BHAGWAN VISHNU

Answer: 1. Matsya, 2. Kurma, 3. Varaha, 4. Narasimha, 5. Vamana 6. Parashurama, 7. Rama, 8. Krishna 9. Buddha, 10. Kalki

### 2. NAME THESE 3 RAMAYANA CHARACTERS

Answers: 1. Lakshman, 2. Sita, 3. Rama

### 3. NAME THESE 4 RAMAYANA CHARACTERS

Answer: 1. Rama, 2. Sita, 3. Lakshman, 4. Surpanakha

### 4. NAME THESE 2 RAMAYANA CHARACTERS

Answers: 1. Sugreeva, 2. Bali

### 5. NAME THESE 6 RAMAYANA CHARACTERS

Answers: 1. Lakshman, 2. Rama, 3. Nala, 4. Neel, 5. Angad, 6. Hanuman

# Notes

# ABOUT THE AUTHOR

**Shantanu Gupta** is an author, TEDx speaker, TV panellist, and the founder of The Ramayana School. He is also a part-time faculty member at Hindu University of America and a professor at Rashtram School of Public Policy, Rishihood University. He is the first to introduce political comic books with his two graphic novels *101 Reasons Why I Will Vote for Modi* and *Ajay to Yogi Adityanath.*

His book *The Monk Who Became Chief Minister*, a biography of Yogi Adityanath, is listed as the 'Most Memorable Nonfiction Books of 2017' by Amazon India, spawning a sequel, *The Monk Who Transformed Uttar Pradesh.* His book *Bharatiya Janata Party: Past, Present and Future* has been translated into multiple Indian languages.

Shantanu has done more than 5,000 TV debates with leading channels such as India Today, CNN News18, Times Now, Republic TV, Aaj Tak, Zee News, India TV, etc. He has written opinion pieces for *The Indian Express, The Hindu, Hindustan Times, The Times of India, Dainik Jagran, Swarajya,* and OpIndia.

Shantanu is a fellow of the University of Oxford's Chevening Gurukul Fellowship. He has an engineering degree from GB Pant University (India), management degree from XLRI, Jamshedpur (India), and a master's in policy and politics from Institute of Development Studies, University of Sussex (United Kingdom). Shantanu has worked for a decade as a process and management consultant in many cities in India, Switzerland, Cyprus, Hungry, and Israel. He has represented India in many international conferences on economy and policy in Germany, Malaysia, and Sri Lanka, and worked with think tanks such as Centre for Civil Society and non-profits such as UNICEF, Naandi Foundation, and National Independent Schools Alliance.